Proceedings of the Sempre MET2014

Researching Music, Education, Technology: Critical Insights

Proceedings of the Sempre MET2014

Researching Music, Education, Technology: Critical Insights

Sempre Conference, 3-4 April 2014

International Music Education Research Centre (iMerc)
Institute of Education
University of London

EDITORS:

Evangelos Himonides
iMerc, Institute of Education, University of London

Andrew King
University of Hull

Proceedings of the Sempre MET2014

Researching Music, Education, Technology: Critical Insights

ISBN: 978-1-905351-29-9

© 2014 Evangelos Himonides & Andrew King

Published in Great Britain in 2014
on behalf of the Society for Education, Music and Psychology Research (Sempre)
by the International Music Education Research Centre (iMerc)
Department of Culture, Communication and Media
Institute of Education
University of London
20, Bedford Way
London WC1H 0AL

copy requests
http://copyrequests.imerc.org

British Library Cataloguing-in-Publication Data

A CIP record is available from the British Library

All rights reserved. Except for the quotation of short passages for the purposes of criticism or review, no part of this publication may be reproduced, stored in a retrieval system, or transmitted, in any form or by any means, electronic, mechanical, photocopying, recording or otherwise, without prior permission from the publisher.

Critical Insights

Researching Music, Education, Technology

Table of Contents

Table of Contents — 7

Keynote address Music technology: production and participation — 13
  Ian Cross

Keynote address Singing synthesis and the Vocal Tract Organ — 15
  David M Howard

Knowledge, Technology and the transformative process in the construction of talking drum (dundun) of the south-west of Nigeria — 23
  Timothy Ajiboye

Online diagnostic measurement of musical abilities in Hungarian schools – a cross-sectional study of 1st to 11th grade students — 25
  Kata Asztalos

Performance Methods for the Interpretation of Tape Music — 29
  Jeremy Baguyos

Michael Meets Ableton Live — 33
  Adam Patrick Bell

Making music with technology: a free improvisation ensemble — 37
  Oded Ben-Tal
  Robert Demianiuk
  Sam Heath
  Sam Kendall
  Diana Salazar

An Imaginary Subject? Designing 'Music & Digital Media' for a Post-Conservatorium BMus Programme — 41
  Samantha Bennett

"The Traveler Sonnet": The technology as a key element in the study of musical heritage through an inter-university and interdisciplinary educational experience   45
Noemy Berbel-Gómez
Alberto Cabedo-Mas
María Elena Riaño-Galán
Cristina Arriaga-Sanz
Maravillas Díaz-Gómez

A brittle discipline: Music Technology and Third Culture Thinking   51
Carola Boehm

Researching coding collaboratively in classrooms: Developing Sonic Pi   55
Pamela Burnard
Samuel Aaron
Alan F. Blackwell

Children's compositional strategies in their interaction with digital tools: a micro-genetic analytical approach   59
Vasiliki Charisi

Influence of sequencing software in musician competences   63
Francisco José Cuadrado Méndez

Preparing the music technology toolbox: addressing the education-industry dilemma   67
Robert Davis
Steven Parker
Paul Thompson

The Art of Practice: the crossroads between reflection, creativity and determination   81
Monica Esslin-Peard
Tony Shorrocks

Initial Teacher Education in England: Music Trainee Teachers' Development of Technology Skills   85
Marina Gall
Nick Breeze

Collaborative music production in a virtual learning environment: An experience with English and Spanish students   89
Andrea Giraldez Hayes
David Carabias Galindo

An Exploratory Study of the Effect of an Eye Guide While
Sight Playing at the Piano 93
Sara Hagen
Walter Boot
Vicki McArthur
Cynthia Stephens-Himonides
Alejandro Cremaschi

Technology-mediated feedback in advanced level piano learning
of ABEGG Variations by Schumann: an exploratory pilot study 99
Luciana Hamond

Musical gameplay: a theoretical exploration 103
Sigrid Jordal Havre
Lauri Väkevä

A constructivist model for opening minds to sound-based music 107
David Holland

Audio Researchers: Are We Not Listening? 111
Andrew Horsburgh

'The old in the new': teaching and learning traditional music
online 115
Ailbhe Kenny

Studio Pedagogy: Perspectives from Producers 119
Andrew King

Introducing technology in Cypriot primary classroom music
lessons: "I learnt using things in music I didn't know existed" 125
Chrysovalentini Konstantinou

The EARS 2 Pedagogical Project – an eLearning environment
to introduce learners to sound-based music 129
Leigh Landy
Sarah Younie
Andrew Hill
Motje Wolf

FourChords Guitar Karaoke Makes Learning Guitar Easy 135
Paula Lehto

Ecocompositional techniques in ubiquitous music practices in
educational settings: Sonic sketching 137
Maria Helena de Lima

Damián Keller
Nuno Otero
Marcelo Soares Pimenta
Victor Lazzarini
Marcelo Johann
Leandro Costalonga

Efficient Computer-Aided Pitch Track and Note Estimation for Scientific Applications . . . 143
Matthias Mauch
Chris Cannam
György Fazekas

Vygotsky, Eliot, and Linguistic Crossroads: Transposing Musical Beauty for the Language Classroom . . . 147
Andrew Meyerhoff

How pianists listen to recordings of Schumann's Träumerei?: Comparisons with self-evaluation and external-evaluation . . . 151
Yuki Morijiri

"I can do it!": Using the iPad in musical performance with students with special needs . . . 155
Clint Randles

Vocalmetrics: exploring multiple dimensions of singing in early popular music recordings . . . 159
Felix Schönfeld
Tilo Hähnel

Processes of Learning in the Project Studio . . . 163
Mark Slater

Picalab Musi-Matemáticas Sonoras Interactivas. Design, implementation and evaluation of a software package and didactic guides for mathematical education based on musical metaphors for primary education in Chile . . . 167
Jesús Tejada
Tomás Thayer
Alicia Venegas
Randall Ledermann
Alberto Lecaros
Mirko Petrovich

Connecting learners, employers and practitioners through emergent digital technology . . . 171
Mark Thorley

How could musicology help me become a better record producer?: tensions between the vocational and the theoretical in music pedagogy   175
   Simon Zagorski-Thomas

Researching Music, Education, Technology

Keynote address
Music technology: production and participation

Ian Cross

University of Cambridge

Abstract

This paper presents a view of music shaped by ethnomusicology and the cognitive sciences, and discusses ways in which culturally-specific models of music have constrained the ways in which music technology has been developed and applied. Almost all contemporary uses of technology in music are grounded in western ideas of music as an autonomous auditory phenomenon. Technology is predominantly used as a tool for manipulating, transforming, producing, disseminating—and analysing—music in the forms described by Turino (2008) as "high fidelity" and "studio audio art", in which music is effectively a product, either audio signal or symbol.

Digital technology has virtualised the creative practice of composing and performing by means of sequencer and performance/production suites (such as *MOTU Digital Performer, Logic Pro, Pro Tools, Ableton Live*, etc.), and the development of dynamic music-oriented programming languages such as *SuperCollider*. Frameworks such as MAX/MSP and *pd* have emerged that allow performers, composers and audiences to dynamically configure the ways in which they can interact with the technology. In all these instances music technology is effectively functioning as a prosthesis, extending the humanly-possible range of ways of engaging with—producing, transforming, and consuming—music. Digital technology has also enabled our knowledge and understanding of music as symbol and as sound to be extended radically. Studies of music corpora have provided new insights into the structures and processes underlying musical pieces, forms and genres. Over the last 20 years or so, Computational Music Analysis and Music Information Retrieval (MIR) has improved dramatically in functionality so as to enhance our understanding of music not only in symbolic, score form but also as audio signal.

However, current applications of technology in music remain firmly oriented towards the treatment of what Turino has described as "presentational" music. As a presentational medium, music is a product of specialised activities (composing, performing) and is primarily to be engaged with through listening. Music's social value for contemporary Western societies has inevitably been moulded by technology; for example, recording has enabled music to become a discrete product with exchange value and with novel economic and political utilities, and digital sampling has become a means of constructing new social liaisons and identities through appropriating and resituating musical sounds. Music is intrinsically a social phenomenon; it has identity and value as music by virtue of the ways in which it is embedded in the categories and values of a culture, as *sound, behaviour* and *concept* (after Merriam, 1963). And presentational music is only one possible cultural manifestation of music; it can be counterpointed with participatory music, where musical activity is not specialised, and where the appropriate mode of engagement in music is not "passive" listening but active participation in music-making.

Music as a participatory medium is under-explored in technological terms. Almost all interactive music systems remain largely focused on the generation of music by a single user; technology is yet to be employed to mediate participatory music-making between groups of users. I shall suggest that this gap arises in part from the prevalence of presentational models of music, and in part because of the absence of models of how people make music together that are capable of being deployed in technological interventions. I shall briefly present some recent work in Cambridge that explores the dynamics of music as interactive process and that applies technology in the mediation of musical interaction.

REFERENCES

Casey, M. A., Veltkamp, R., Goto, M., Leman, M., Rhodes, C., & Slaney, M. (2008). Content-based music information retrieval: Current directions and future challenges. *Proceedings of the IEEE*, 96(4), 668–696.

Merriam, A. P. (1963). Purposes of ethnomusicology, an anthropological view. *Ethnomusicology*, 7(3), 206–213.

Turino, T. (2008). *Music as social life: The politics of participation*. University of Chicago Press.

Critical Insights

Keynote address
Singing synthesis and the Vocal Tract Organ

‖ David M Howard

Centre for Singing Science, Audio Lab,
Department of Electronics, University of York

Abstract

Vocal synthesis has been the subject of investigation since the late 18th century when von Kempelen produced his mechanical 'speaking machine'. The advert of electronics has enabled a number of different methods of voice synthesis to be realized in practice. Recently with the advent of 3-D printing and magnetic resonance imaging of human vocal tracts, it has been possible to create synthetic vocal sounds that combine both mechanical (3-D printed tracts) and electronic (synthesized larynx sound source) to enable the effects of various parts of the vocal tract on the acoustic output to be investigated. Given that the 3-D tracts look rather like organ pipes, the author (an organist) has developed a new musical instrument based on this technology, which is called the Vocal Tract Organ. This paper reviews voice synthesis techniques and describes the structure and operation of the Vocal Tract Organ.

Human voice synthesis

The human voice production system consists of three elements [1]: the power source (breathing), the sound source (the vibrating vocal folds in the larynx for pitched sung sounds) and the sound modifiers (the varying resonant acoustic properties of the tubes of the throat, mouth and nose above the larynx). For the purposes of considering voice synthesis, only the sound source and sound modifiers are relevant since the power source for electronic voice synthesis is electrical rather than air flowing from the lungs.

One of the earliest examples of a speech synthesiser is Baron Von Kempelen's "speaking machine" in the 1790s. This was a mechanical model of the human speech production system, which was "played" by a human operator. An original exists in the Deutsches Museum in Munich and the author's modern replica is shown in figure 1. Its power source is the under-arm bellows, its sound source is a vibrating reed and its sound modifiers is the leather tube controlled by hand representing the mouth. In addition, it has additional outputs for the production of the consonants in 'sea' and 'she'.

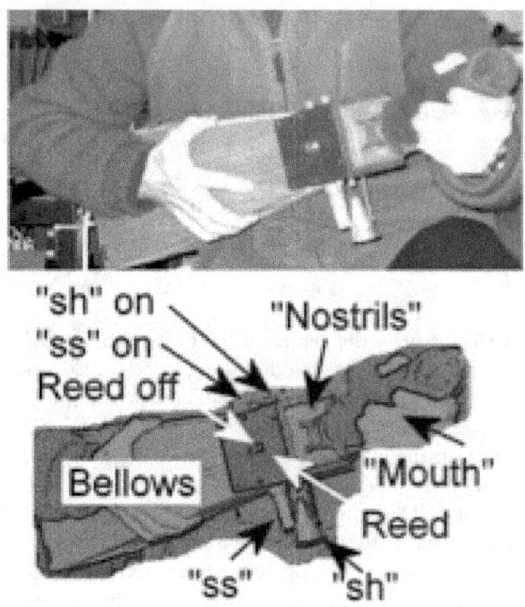

Figure 1: The author's replica Von Kempelen machine (top) and labelled version (bottom).

With the advent of electronics, a number of different approaches have been adopted for electronic speech synthesis ranging from modifying natural speech recordings to direct modelling of the physiological processes involved in speaking. Styger and Keller [2] provide a useful summary of speech synthesis methods under four categories shown in table 1. These approaches are analysed on the basis of two scales using a star rating in the table:

- (A) *flow of control parameters* (the required sampling rate), and
- (B) *model complexity* (speech production knowledge required).

For the manipulation of natural speech waveforms (1), the required *control parameters* are at a maximum of once per fundamental period, but the *model complexity* is at a minimum. For vocal tract articulatory physical modelling (4) the required *control parameters* are at a minimum of once per articulatory gesture, but the *model complexity* is at a maximum requiring detailed knowledge of vocal tract articulation.

#	Category	control parameters	model complexity
1	Manipulation of natural speech waveforms *no knowledge of speech production mechanism*	****	*
2	Linear predictive synthesis *all-pole acoustic model of the vocal tract*	***	**
3	Formant synthesis *formant parameters are varied*	**	***
4	Vocal tract articulatory physical modelling *control of articulation itself*	*	****

Table 1: Organisation of speech synthesis methods by from Styger and Keller [2] in terms of the *flow of control parameters* and *model complexity* to illustrate key differences between available methods.

Typical experiences with today's electronic voice synthesis are that they can produce a highly *intelligible* speech output, but that it is rare if ever that an electronically synthesized voice based on methods 2-4 is mistaken as having emerged from a human vocal tract. Few if any of today's synthesizers are able to produce a *natural* sounding speech output. Formant synthesis (3) is the most commonly used method and it has been used for a long time [2-4], which is based directly on the source/filter model [5] of speech production.

The "Festival" system [6-7], in which recorded speech waveforms are manipulated to create connected speech, is a popular basis for electronic speech synthesis. The key issue is keeping the joins transparent to the listeners

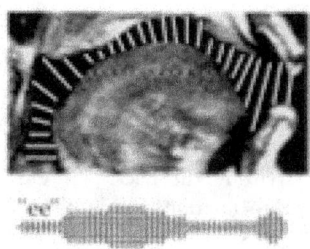

Figure 2: Magnetic resonance image of the vowel "ee" and its 2-D waveguide mesh representation (the larynx is on the left and the lips on the right).

Synthesis based on vocal tract articulatory physical modelling (4 in table 1) recreates vocal tract articulation behaviour to simulate directly the process of speaking itself, rather than the sounds it generates. Sound is created via physical modelling of acoustic pressure in the vocal tract with an appropriately placed sound source input for pitched and non-pitched sounds. Physical modelling of acoustic pressure in the vocal tract was first based on the 1-D digital waveguide [8], and it can be extended to 2-D or 3-D [9-10], but the computation load increases rapidly, making the running of a 3-D model impossible now in real-time on today's PCs (up to an 1 hour's processing can be required for 1 second of speech output). A magnetic resonance image (MRI) for the vowel "ee" along with its waveguide mesh layout is shown in figure 2; note that the larynx is on the left and the lips on the right.

THE VOCAL TRACT ORGAN

The vocal tract is a tube and a visual link with the pipes of a pipe organ is readily made, despite the bend in the vocal tract. In particular, it has the potential to challenge the *Vox Humana* stop that is found in a number of large pipe organs, but which typically sounds most unlike the human voice! The complete 3-D vocal tract dimensions can be measured from an MRI session based on a set of MRI pictures taken across the vocal tract. From these a 3-D print can be created of the vocal tract, which will be an accurate representation of whatever sound was being articulated (and held steady for around 16 seconds) in the MRI scanner. If the larynx end of the 3-D print is set up to couple with a suitable loudspeaker, it can be made to sound if an appropriate larynx sound source excitation is provided to the loudspeaker. An example 3-D print coupled to a loudspeaker drive unit (Adastra 952.210) is shown in figure 3.

The prototype Vocal Tract Organ consists of six 3-D printed Vocal Tracts for the same vowel, but with slightly different lengths (each differs from its neighbour by 2.5 mm to ensure that the outputs are not absolutely identical) with their loudspeaker drivers. Each printed vocal tract can be made to sound if a suitable voice source signal is applied at the position of the larynx in the neck [1]. The larynx sound source waveform is a close approximation to that observed from the vibrating vocal folds, and its practical implementation is based on the Liljencrants/Fant (LF) glottal source model [11], which is synthesised in practice using Pure Data, or PD, [12]. PD is well suited to this because it enables a wavetable synthesiser to be implemented that is based on either one cycle that is either (a) calculated from a set of harmonic amplitudes (a pulse and a sawtooth waveform is available in the system that is based on these; the user can switch between them), or (b) drawn by hand using the mouse (this is how the LF model is implemented enabling changes to its shape to be easily tested). The implementation of this glottal source for the Vocal Tract Organ for multi-part, or *polyphonic*, synthesis is described in [13]. In order that the result is perceived as being close to a natural output, each channel has a separate setting for vibrato rate, vibrato depth and volume. An overall volume control is also included which can be set using the mouse and a slider or externally manipulated via a MIDI control parameter. These can be set independently either via an on-screen slider with the mouse or over MIDI (Musical Instrument Digital Interface) via any programmable MIDI controller device. The organ is played via a MIDI keyboard.

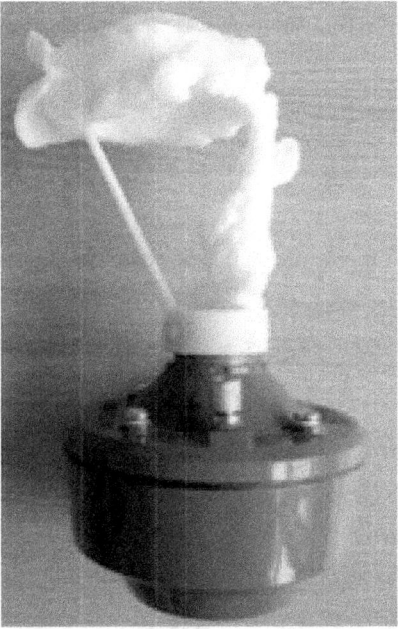

Figure 3: A 3-D print for the vowel "ah" sitting atop its loudspeaker drive unit as used in the Vocal Tract Organ.

Four-part chorale style music can be played on the Vocal Tract Organ (quasi soprano, alto, tenor, bass, or SATB), an implementing 6-channels means that there are two spare channels to 'catch' additional notes during *legato* playing between chords. Clearly this could be changed as appropriate to performance needs. The six audio outputs are routed to the loudspeaker drivers via an RME Fireface 400 multi-channel digital to analogue converter, via six amplifiers.

The author composed two pieces to demonstrate the Vocal Tract Organ, specifically to enable its output to be compared directly with live singers. In the first, a barbershop-style vocalize called *Vocal Vision II*, two male singers sing two parts and two other parts are played on the Vocal Tract Organ. A performance of *Vocal Vision II* can be seen and heard on YouTube [10]. In the second, the Vocal Tract Organ accompanies a solo soprano singing an opera aria. The original stimulus for this was a black-tie after-dinner event in the presence of a member of a member of the British Royal Family for which a short *flash mob* opera aria was required highlighting an advance in engineering in a musical context. *O mio babbino caro* (Puccini) was sung by a mezzo-soprano, for which a new chorale-like keyboard accompaniment was created. Filming was not allowed at the first performance, but it was at a second a few weeks later and this can be viewed on YouTube [11] (from 2m50s following a brief presentation about the organ).

CONCLUSIONS

Vocal synthesis is highly intelligible but typically non-natural and likely to be improved by moving towards computed models of articulation inhuman voice production. Such models are based on magnetic resonance imaging of the vocal tract, which provides images that can be 3-D printed. These 3-D prints look like organ pipes, and when placed on suitable loudspeakers drivers, they can be made to sound like the vowels of the original speaker. A Vocal Tract Organ has been developed that uses a set of such 3-D prints; a modern-day *Vox Humana* organ stop that offers new possibilities for music performance.

ACKNOWLEDGEMENTS

The author thanks the staff at the York Neuroimaging Centre for their help in capturing the images, and Pete Turner for help with the 3-D print creation and electronic implementation of the Vocal Tract Organ.

REFERENCES

[1] Howard, D.M., and Murphy, (2008)., Plural Press, San Diego.

[2] Styger, T., and Keller, E. (1994). Formant synthesis, In: *Fundamentals of speech synthesis and speech recognition*, Keller, E. (Ed.), Chichester: John Wiley and Sons, 109-128.

[3] Holmes, W.J., and Holmes, J.N., (2002). *Speech synthesis and recognition*, London: CRC Press.

[4] Klatt, D.H. (1980). Software for a cascade/parallel formant synthesizer, *Journal of the Acoustical Society of America*, 67, (3), 971-995.

[5] Fant, G. (1960). *The acoustic theory of speech production*, The Hague: Mouton.

[6] Taylor, P.A., Black, A., and Caley, R. (1998). The architecture of the festival speech synthesis system, in *Proc. 3rd ESCA Workshop in Speech Synthesis*, Jenolan Caves, Australia, 147–151.

[7] WWW-1: http://www.cstr.ed.ac.uk/projects/festival/ (last accessed 11th March 2014)

[8] J. L. Kelly and C. C. Lochbaum, (1962). Speech synthesis, in *Proceedings of the 4th International Congress on Acoustics*, Copenhagen, Denmark, 1–4.

[9] Mullen, J., Howard, D.M., and Murphy, D.T. (2006). Waveguide Physical Modeling of Vocal Tract Acoustics: Improved Formant Bandwidth Control from Increased Model Dimensionality, *IEEE Transactions on Speech and Audio Processing*, 14, (3), 964-971.

[10] Mullen, J. Murphy, D.T. and Howard D.M. (2007). Real-time dynamic articulations in the 2D waveguide mesh vocal tract model, *IEEE Transactions on Speech and Audio Processing*, 15, 2, 577-585.

[11] Fant. G., Liljencrants, J., and Lin, Q. G.: A four-parameter model of glottal flow, STL-QPSR, 2, (3), 119-156, (1985)

[12] WWW-1: http://www.puredata.info (last accessed 11th March 2014)

[13] Howard, D.M., Daffern, H., and Brereton, J.: Four-part choral synthesis system for investigating intonation in a cappella choral singing, Logopedics Phoniatrics Vocology, 38, (3), 135-142, (2013)

[14] WWW-3: http://www.youtube.com/watch?v=pUryWk-s9Ig (last accessed 11th March 2014)

[15] WWW-4: http://www.youtube.com/watch?v=SX-f1oU0_Kk (last accessed 11th March 2014)

Knowledge, Technology and the transformative process in the construction of talking drum (dundun) of the south-west of Nigeria

▌ Timothy Ajiboye

The Polytechnic, Ibadan, Oyo State, Nigeria

Abstract

The advancement of technology in the present generation has been of greater impact in all areas of studies. The construction of musical instruments is an aspect of music technology that deals with practical demonstration and application of tools, machines and materials. Talking drum (dundun) from the south-west of Nigeria being the most popular indigenous musical instrument, has witness various transformation in its construction process and design. Nigerian traditional musical instruments certainly need improvement in terms of appearance and techniques in its construction process. It is in line with this objective that this paper emphasizes on the technological transformative process in the construction of talking drum (dundun) of the south-west Nigerian. Transformative theory was adopted and data was gathered using observation, interview and participant-observation methods. However, the finding of the paper reveals that the innovative attempt intended to encourage the development of new forms of traditional instruments, based on aesthetics, may be of a standard in time to come. In conclusion, the paper argues that the transformation proposed in the outlook of the musical instrument from its antique to modern form is a new example to follow. The paper recommends the use of modern techniques, tools and materials in the construction of traditional musical instruments using technological devices is quite promising and should be encouraged.

Keywords

Transformative, Innovative, Technology

Aims

Aim of this paper is to emphasizes the use of modern technological devices inthe construction of talking drum (dundun) of the south-west Nigerian to witnes the tranformative process of new apprearance in terms of new techniques in its construction process in developing new form of traditional instrument based on good aesthetics and of good standard.

Methods

Transformative theory was adopted and data was gathered using observation, interview and participant-observation methods.

Outcomes

The paper recommends the use of modern techniques, tools and materials in the construction of traditional musical instruments using technological devices is quite promising and should be encouraged.

Epilogue

Knowledge, technology and the tranformative process in the construction of talking drum (dundun) of the south-west of nigeria.

References

Edet E.M. (1967) 'Music education in Nigeria' notes on education and research in Africa music, *No. 1 University of Ghana*, Legon, No. 1. Pp 38-54.

Okonkwo V. N. (2009) 'comparative Assessment of Music Education practice in Nigeria and selected global Experiences'. *Journal of the Association of Nigeria Musicologists*, No.3. pp.40

Online diagnostic measurement of musical abilities in Hungarian schools – a cross-sectional study of 1st to 11th grade students

▌ Kata Asztalos

University of Szeged Doctoral School of Education, Magyarország

Abstract

This study describes the potential of applying online test for the diagnostic measurement of musical abilities. Recent tendencies of education internationally show that technology based assessment has an increasingly important role. In our research an online test battery was developed and implemented (N=2961) in primary and secondary schools. The test was administered the eDia online assessment platform and consist of 73 closed (multiple and alternative choice) questions. We examined the developmental tendencies of rhythm, tempo, pitch, harmony, dynamics, timbre discrimination and one task measured the ability of visual connection. Test recording was carried out in classrooms equipped with computers and headphones. Results indicate that the test difficulty fitted well to the ability level of students, and the majority of the sample found the test interesting. Correlations were found between test achievement and music related activities. Model fit values of the structural equitation modeling supported the theoretical models of musical processing. The results of the present study encourage further research to explore the potentials of computer-based musical testing and developmental processes in music classrooms.

Keywords

technology-based musical ability research, development of musical abilities, online diagnostic testing, assessment of musical abilities

AIMS

Primary goal of the research is to develop a useful diagnostic tool for music classrooms, which is broadly accessible and easy to use and administer. We also aimed to take the advantages of online testing in contrast to the traditional paper and pencil tests and to arouse students' interest and help maintain motivation. The aims of the present study are to explore the potentials of online assessment, to outline the developmental trends and structural model of the measured musical abilities and to analyze their relationship with background variables.

THEORETICAL BACKGROUND

For developing the online measurement tool we applied items measuring musical hearing abilities regardless of previous experience or musical literacy. To define these abilities we applied the cognitive models of music processing (Peretz & Coltheart, 2003; Koelsch, 2013) and the models of musical abilities (Hargreaves, 2012). Based on these works tasks were created for the measurement of temporal organization (rhythm and tempo discrimination) and melodic organization (pitch, harmony and melody discrimination). As our aim was to cover the holistic system of musical parameters, we supplemented the framework with tasks of timbre, dynamics, tonality hearing and visual connection.

METHODS

Participants of the study were primary and secondary school students (N=2961) from 1st to 11th grade, selected from different areas of Hungary. The test was administered through the eDia online assessment platform which was developed for delivering diagnostic tests. This way of testing provides opportunities for several innovative features impossible to realize with paper and pencil tests. Audio assistance may helps students with reading difficulties to understand the instructions. Online testing provides an opportunity to start music stimuli when students are totally prepared to hear them and to listen to them, thus everybody can answer the questions at their pace. Further advantage is that the volume can be changed by individual needs. Students completed the test in classrooms equipped with computers and headphones. There was no time limit for the individual tasks but students were not allowed to return to the previous items. The test consisted of alternative and multiple choice closed questions. Each item is worth one point, maximum score was 73. Cronbach's alpha shows growing tendency for the 11 age groups, between .666 (1st grade) and .891 (10th grade). The test items were followed by a short questionnaire asking students' opinion about the testing itself and their music related habits and activities.

OUTCOMES

Data were imported from the eDia platform for further SPSS and MPlus analysis. Distribution of the results indicates that the difficulty of the test was appropriate for the measured age groups. The lowest test achievement was reached by 1st graders (M=47.44, SD=9.45) and the highest by 11th graders (M=71.26, SD=13.54). According to the judgment of students, 50.8% found the test interesting and 28.9% moderately interesting. 46.7% thought that achieved well on the tasks. A modest correlation was found between the two variables above (r=.224, p<.01) and between students' estimated and real achievement (r=.134, p<.01). Results do not show significant differences between boys and girls. Test score correlate positively with music related activities like the frequency of listening to music (r=.184, p<.01), learning on an instrument (r=.233, p<.01), having a musical instrument at home (r=.190, p<.01), years of studying an instrument (r=.440, p<.01) and frequency of playing an instrument (r=.343, p<.01). To analyze the dimensions and structure of musical abilities a confirmatory factor analysis was carried out (RMSEA=.072, CFI=.966, TLI=.933, SRMR=.027). Factors are mostly in accordance with the models of musical processing (processing of temporal features, melody contour, frequency and qualitative features of musical phenomena).

IMPLICATION

A general problem is that the current forms of musical assessment are highly subjective and informal; using objective tests in classrooms can provide reliable information for the participants of the educational process. Furthermore in those countries where school monitoring is frequent, subjects outside of this process receive less attention. Enrichment of the assessment culture could be a solution for these problems. The technology-based musical ability test could be a useful supplement to high-quality music pedagogical work and the diagnostic information allows targeted developmental work even in the case of large class sizes. Further analyses are required to establish the effects of cognitive and school-related background variables on test achievement and to explore the potentials of computer based assessment of musical abilities.

Acknowledgements

This research was supported by the European Union and the State of Hungary, co-financed by the European Social Fund in the framework of TÁMOP-4.2.4.A/ 2-11/1-2012-0001 'National Excellence Program'.

References

Hargreaves, D. J. (2012). Musical imagination: Perception and production, beauty and creativity. *Psychology of Music*, 40. 5. 539–557.

Koelsch, S. (2013). *Music and Brain*. John Wiley and Sons Ltd., West Sussex, UK

Peretz, I. & Coltheart, M. (2003). Modularity of Music Processing. *Nature Neuroscience*, 6. 7, 688–691.

Critical Insights

Performance Methods for the Interpretation of Tape Music

▌ Jeremy Baguyos

    University of Nebraska (Omaha), United States of America

ABSTRACT

One of the dilemmas facing the Electroacoustic performer is the lack of a methodology for the interpretation of tape compositions with live performer. *Performance Methods for the Interpretation of Tape Music* discusses some methods that a performer can use to interpret and communicate an Electroacoustic musical gesture to an audience. Some of the methods are drawn from materials that the composers themselves have outlined in the literature that accompanies the recordings of classic Electroacoustic works like Davidovsky's *Synchronisms* and Druckman's *Synapse_Valentine*. In the pursuit of an emerging performance method for live musicians with tape, the most fundamental charge for the performer is the following: to identify the nature of the musical relationship between the electronics and performer and clearly delineate the relationship in the live performance realization. There are three basic considerations in the identification and delineation of the gestural relationship between tape electronics and live performer: rhythmic integration, juxtaposition, and timbre integration.

KEYWORDS

electroacoustic, tape, performance

AIMS

Conservatory training is the traditional route for most performers in the preparation for a music performance career in classical music, but Electroacoustic music is usually not part of that training. One of the problems is the lack of an established and uniformly accepted methodology for the interpretation of tape with live performers. In the pursuit of an emerging performance method for live musicians with tape, the most fundamental charge for the performer is the following: to identify the nature of the musical relationship between the electronics and performer and clearly delineate the relationship in the live performance realization. There are three basic considerations in the identification and delineation of the gestural relationship between tape electronics and live performer: rhythmic integration, juxtaposition, and timbre integration.

METHODS

The aspect of rhythmic integration for purposes of defining the relationship between electronics and live performer is best illustrated in Davidovsky's *Synchronisms*. These works are described by Davidovsky as "a series of short pieces wherein conventional instruments are used in conjunction with electronic sounds" and "to achieve integration of both into a coherent musical texture" (Composers Recordings 1966). In the *Synchronisms*, especially Nos. 1, 2, 3, 5, and 6, Davidovsky demonstrates a wide variety of formats for rhythmic integration between the machine and the human performer. The rhythmic integration can consist of occasional clock timings that require coordination between tape and performer only at certain junctions in the music, which leaves the performer plenty of freedom to exercise rubato in his own part. This is the practice for the performer in *Synchronisms* No. 1. The other end of the spectrum is *Synchronisms* No. 6, which requires total, controlled interaction between the tape and performer. The score is notated with precise indications resulting in a highly integrated work with almost no performer control (Soule 1978). In any piece of electronic music, the performer must identify the level of rhythmic integration, and respond accordingly with rubato, tight ensemble, or something in between. The theme of juxtaposition is illustrated in the works of Jacob Druckman. Druckman outlined a useful tool with compositions like *Animus III* and *Synapse_Valentine* when they were recorded on the same disk under the organizing principle of the juxtaposition of electronics and human performer. *Animus III* and *Synapse_/Valentine* represent two "polar possibilities of combinations of live and prerecorded sound" (Nonesuch 1971). In *Animus III*, the clarinet sounds from the human performer and the tape sound are "inextricably combined." In *Synapse_Valentine* "the electronic and the live are juxtaposed, but completely separate" (Nonesuch 1971). Chamber musicians often use the technique of thinking of a dialogue between parts or that the different instruments are having a conversation. This is similar to the idea of juxtaposition between tape and performer. It could result in the "gradual dissolution of the personality of the player" as in *Animus III* (Druckman 1978). On the other hand, it can be elegantly juxtaposed in *Synapse_/Valentine*. In the same way that dialogue between parts is a fundamental issue in the rehearsal and music criticism of an orchestra performance, interaction and dialogue between parts becomes a staring point in the interpretation and appreciation of tape music. It is the obligation of the performer to find this starting point in the continuum outlined by Druckman. Juxtaposition can be conceived in a more traditional sense. For example, "If electronic sounds are used with a symphonic ensemble as direct contrasts to the conventional instrumental sounds, the work can be much like the baroque concerto grosso. Either one of the sound groups can act as concertino or concerto" (Luening 1989). In an emerging performance method, it is the performer's role to recognize when the composer is attempting a juxtaposition and to delineate that contrast as if a baroque orchestra was delineating the concertino in one of the Brandenburg Concertos. This can be applied to a variety of works such as *Correspondences* by Milton Babbitt and *Déserts* by Edgard Varèse. Timbre integration in the same soundspace has been discussed and utilized by composers. Dexter Morrill pointed out the possibilities in that "compositions that feature timbres similar to those of live performers have a potential for balance that might not otherwise exist" (Morrill 1989). He promoted the idea of a "confusion between real and synthetic sound sources." In his composition *Studies* for trumpet and tape, Morrill "found it important to have the loudspeakers elevated to the height of the trumpet bell and to have both the loudspeakers and the player a good distance from the audience" (Morrill 1989). One interpretive tool that performers can use, then, is to recognize and delineate in performance, the timbre blend created by the effective orchestration of the computer and the human performer. This can be done through proper mixing of levels, correct loudspeaker placement, and performer control. A tape piece that demonstrates the notion of a live performer effectively becoming part of the texture of the tape part is the classic *Philomel* by Milton Babbitt. In this work the punctuating, disjunct entrances of the soprano sound like the punctuating, disjunct entrances of the RCA Mark II. In this tape piece and other tape pieces the live musician is to blend with the tape and seamlessly become part of the texture of the tape. In orchestration, a composer can combine two instruments to create one texture. It is the conductor's or performer's job to recognize that intent and to make sure that the two timbres are communicated as one timbre in the texture of the music.

Outcomes

As the Electroacoustic genre continues to mature, the methodologies of interpretation, performance, and appreciation of the genre will emerge and mature as well. Part of the genesis of this methodology includes the pursuit of an emerging performance method for live musicians with tape with the following fundamental considerations for identifying and delineating the relationship of the electronics with the live performer: rhythmic integration, juxtaposition, and timbre blend.

OPEN DISCUSSION

The author has conducted panel discussions about the performance of electroacoustic music and is open to questions, comments, and discussion from other scholars and practitioners in the area of performance.

ACKNOWLEDGEMENTS

University of Nebraska at Omaha College of Information Science and Technology and College of Communication, Fine Arts & Media

REFERENCES

Morrill, Dexter (1989). "Loudspeakers and Performers: Some Problems and Proposals." In *On the Wires of Our Nerves*, edited by Robin Julian Heifetz (London and Toronto: Associated University Presses, 1989. First published in *Computer Music Journal* 5, No. 4 (Winter 1981): 25-29.

Nonesuch (1971). Liner notes for Jacob Druckman, *Synapse_Valentine*. Nonesuch H-71253.

Soule, Richard C. (1978). "*Synchronisms* Nos. 1, 2, 3, 5, and 6 of Mario Davidovsky: A Style Analysis." DMA diss., Peabody Conservatory of Johns Hopkins University.

Michael Meets Ableton Live

▌ Adam Patrick Bell

Montclair State University, United States

ABSTRACT

Using a case study method entailing video-based observations, semi-structured interviews, and screen recordings, this article presents the making and learning processes of 53-year-old Michael as he navigates using the digital audio workstation Ableton Live for the first time. Drawing on his past experiences with analog recording technologies, Michael utilizes the skeuomorphic cues built into Ableton in a self-directed trial and error approach to learning. The purpose of the study was to examine how Michael integrates recording technology (e.g., Ableton Live) into his music-making practices and to demonstrate his adoption and integration of a skillset typically associated with the domain of audio engineering autodidactically.

KEYWORDS

home recording, digital audio workstation, autodidacticism

AIMS

With the rise of home recording and the ubiquitous use of DAWs in home (project) studios, how are the skills typically associated with audio engineering used and learned by the musician? The purpose of this study was to examine how recording technologies, especially digital audio workstations (DAWs), are used by musicians in the home recording environment. To examine this hybridized role in which a single individual is responsible for writing, performing, recording, and mixing his or her own works, a case study model was adopted to document the making and learning processes of Michael, a 53-year-old Brooklyn-based guitarist.

METHODS

Drawing on Stake (1995) and Eisner (1998), an interpretive research paradigm was adopted to conduct a qualitative case study using the ethnographic tools of semi-structured interviews, observations (using video recordings and screen recordings), and stimulated recall interviews (using selected video excerpts). Over the course of three months, Michael engaged in his typical practice of music-making with a Digital Audio Workstation (DAW) and recorded this process with a video camera (Aiptek T7) and screen recording software (QuickTime). As a means of observation, video captured the working processes of Michael in his home studio, a strategy previously utilized in studies with a similar approach to data collection (Daniel, 2006; King, 2008; Seddon & Biasutti, 2010). The thick description video analysis procedure outlined by Goldman (2007) was employed to describe Michael's processes, gestures, interactions, events, and actions that occurred outside of the DAW environment. Adopting the approach of Mellor (2008) and Tobias (2010), screen recording documented a "play-by-play" of Michaels' actions within the DAW. Additionally, Michael participated in a semi-structured interview for every 10 hours of video he recorded. Interviews about a specific session were scheduled as close as possible to the date of the session to maximize memory recall. In total, Michael recorded approximately 20 hours of video and 20 hours of screen recordings simultaneously. Further, he participated in two semi-structured interviews, each lasting 2 hours, and a two-hour stimulated recall interview. For all data sources (interviews, videos, screen recordings), the guiding principle of analysis was to examine how Michael used recording technology to make music and document both his making and learning processes.

OUTCOMES

Michael has never received a formal lesson in recording; anything he knows about audio engineering he taught himself by reading a manual or through trial and error. Certainly his pedigree of recording experience in professional studios must have had some implicit influence on his recording knowledge and skills—learning by osmosis—but Michael makes no such claim. His greatest teacher was himself. Theoretically Michael is not expected to exhibit traits of the Web 2.0 learner by virtue of the fact that he is not a "millennial," but he is a consummate self-directed trial and error learner. It may be the case that a dependency on trial and error techniques is characteristic of learners reared in the computer age, but Michael's learning history helps to illustrate Waksman's (2004) assertion that there is a lineage of trial and error learning with music technology ("tinkering") that predates home computing. Michael's self-directed trial and error learning strategies were carried over from his analog experiences when he emigrated to his new digital devices, largely aided by the cues of skeuomorphic design. For example, discussing his entry into using Pro Tools, Michael professed, "I didn't have anybody tutoring me and I didn't have any help files, so I just had to figure it out for myself." Despite the bounty of online resources and sheer number of people engaged in the practice of home recording, Michael chooses to go it alone. Click and consequence composition, a modern adaptation of the trial and error descriptor, best characterizes Michael's approach to music-making with a DAW. Michael is an experimental-oriented music-maker, he labors to make singular sounds. He used Ableton to tinker with timbres, stumbling across sounds that he deemed "cool," and "outstanding and strange." Michael's aural expeditions entailed expectant encounters of unearthing new sounds: he knew he'd find something; he just wasn't sure what it would be. Scrolling through sounds, he employed the click and consequence method, auditioning sounds until he at last found the din of his dreams.

DISCUSSION

Michael is a particularly interesting case because he has had hands-on experience with the leading recording technologies over the last four decades. He has lived through and adapted to the technological advances in recording. Further, Michael has maintained a home recording studio throughout his career, while continuing to record in professional studios for other artists. He estimates that he has appeared on 72 recordings, but this tally does not include his own recordings, of which he says: "Mostly those were for my own edification to be honest with you. I'm inspired to do so and I will always record my own music at home." When Michael makes music in his home studio there is no rush, no deadline, and no impetus to distribute his music to the masses. Michael perceives his studio as a retreat from a traditional studio system that dictates decisions. In his home studio he feels unimpeded: free to explore and make unconventional decisions that are not inhibited by an overbearing audio engineer. Considering Michael's history of being a professional touring musician, I suspect the allure of having an album to market has lost its luster to some extent. Alternatively, he derives satisfaction from living on a musical island unencumbered by the demands of record labels, managers, band members, engineers, and producers. The Internet enables Michael to circumvent the distribution network of the record industry, he can easily post his music online, but he chooses not to. This is an inaction of passivity more than aversion. Quite simply, he is not concerned with attracting an audience. His music is his music, and that seems to be sufficient for him. Michael uses his secluded studio to perform almost exclusively for himself. From an early age, Michael engaged in recording his own songs and musical ideas with a makeshift multi-track recorder. He became very adept at mixing his own music and is keenly aware of mixing techniques and their impact on the overall sound of a recording. Engaging with recording technology is a constant theme that runs through Michael's life. He uses it frequently, methodically, and enthusiastically. A final product is not necessary for Michael to feel that his time is well spent; the act of recording is in and of itself a gratifying pursuit.

ACKNOWLEDGEMENTS

The Social Sciences and Humanities Research Council of Canada

REFERENCES

Waksman, S. (2004). California noise: Tinkering with hardcore and heavy metal in southern California. *Social Studies of Science*, 34(5), 675-702.

Tobias, E. (2010). *Crossfading and plugging in: Secondary students' engagement and learning in a songwriting and technology class*. (Doctoral Dissertation, Northwestern University). Available from ProQuest Dissertations and Theses database (UMI No. 3402496).

King, A. (2008). Collaborative learning in the music studio. *Music Education Research*, 10(3), 423-438.

Making music with technology: a free improvisation ensemble

▌ Oded Ben-Tal
   Kingston University, United Kingdom

▌ Robert Demianiuk
   Kingston University, United Kingdom

▌ Sam Heath
   Kingston University, United Kingdom

▌ Sam Kendall
   Kingston University, United Kingdom

▌ Diana Salazar
   City University London, United Kingdom

Abstract

In 2011 four staff members at the music department of Kingston university (Drs. Diana Salazar, Louise Harris, John Ferguson, Oded Ben-Tal) came together to establish an electronic ensemble – KUDAC (Kingston University Digital Arts Collective). The ensemble brings staff and students together for weekly 'musicking' with technology – ranging from traditional instruments, to computers, to hacked circuit boards. A central element of the ensemble from its inception is a democratic approach – we explore the musical possibilities and challenges together and gradually mould our practice through a free exchange. This presentation will consider the role of the ensemble within the specific context of our music department, provide the perspective of both staff and students about the working of the ensemble and its relation to individual and collective practice, and explore the challenges and opportunities our approach offers for music technology education.

KEYWORDS

improvisation, creativity, ensemble performance

AIMS

An important aspect of Kudac from its inception is the focus on creative exploration in relation to staff research interests. This exposed students directly to staff research and, perhaps even more valuably, to research development. Much of the creative engagement of students in a music technology course, regardless of the particular musical style, revolves around working, mostly alone, in a studio. This activity excludes two important components of music education – music as a performance art and the social, collaborative aspect of music. Especially for students who arrive at university without a traditional grounding in instrumental performance, the opportunity to make music in an ensemble contributes to their understanding of music, music making, and musical culture. On the individual level students gradually develop their own instrument or instrumental approach to technology.

METHODS

The development of the ensemble entails weekly sessions. Some sessions, particularly at the beginning of the year could be devoted to more to learning and development. Unlike some laptop ensembles where all members use the same setup and utilise the same tools, at Kudac we are agnostic about tools and methods encouraging each student to find their own practice based on the set of skills they bring while also offering help learning new tools. Participating in Kudac helps students develop their own musical practice with and through technology while also fostering skills such as listening and evaluating music in order to effectively contribute to a performance. As an ensemble focused on free improvisation and where ideas for structuring individual pieces emerge out of discussion, listening skills (musical and interpersonal) are crucial as is the honing of aesthetic judgements and the ability to act and react effectively to varying contexts.

OUTCOMES

Over these three years Kudac enhanced the educational opportunities within the music department. The positive experience of the first year led us to institute a new first year module which aims to implement a minimal version of the hands-on approach to technology adapted to more formal setting and larger group. Students are asked to develop short technology-based performances in small groups. The ensemble also opened new opportunities within the department across intra-disciplinary boundaries. We were also able to organise exchange concerts with other universities, centred on the work of Kudac, which presented the work done at Kingston to wider audience and exposed Kingston students (and not just participants in the ensemble) to the practices of music technology at other institutions.

Discussion

Maintaining and sustaining such an ensemble does require additional effort which poses a challenge with diminishing resources in many music departments. Traditional ensembles build on (and support) instrumental tuition provided by the department to individuals. In Kudac both need to be provided within the ensemble framework and thus require additional investment on the part of staff. This is particularly important because of the focus on encouraging students to develop their own approach which can also involve additional tools (which other members of the ensemble may not be already familiar with). Technically Kudac requires a fairly elaborate setup – multiple computers plugged into a single sound system. Unlike laptop orchestras that focus the laptop as a portable sound producing instrument we prefer to focus on sound quality offered by good, multichannel speaker setup at the expense of portability. However, Kudac encourages students to learn new technology tools or to apply the tools they often use in radically different ways thus opening new ways of conceptualising music including how music can be created and presented.

References

Wang, G., Trueman, D., Smallwood, S., & Cook, P. R. (2008). The laptop orchestra as classroom. *Computer Music Journal*, 32(1), 26-37.

Bown, O., Eldridge, A., & Mccormack, J. (2009). Understanding Interaction in Contemporary Digital Music: from instruments to behavioural objects. *Organised Sound*, 14(02), 188-196.

Jordà, S. (2002). Improvising with computers: A personal survey (1989–2001). *Journal of New Music Research*, 31(1), 1-10.

An Imaginary Subject? Designing 'Music & Digital Media' for a Post-Conservatorium BMus Programme

Samantha Bennett

The Australian National University, Australia

Abstract

As a stand-alone course or module in a wider programme context, the emerging topic of 'Music & Digital Media' is taught in few institutions worldwide. Harvard Law School[1] focuses on legal, business and distribution content, building on the copyright management issues faced by global music industry governing bodies.[2] The University of Newcastle, Australia,[3] offers 'Music & Digital Media' as being the practice-led creation of multimedia content across a variety of applications. These quite different understandings demonstrate the breadth of potential topic scope under an indiscernible and fluid heading. A framework for 'Music & Digital Media' was authored as part of the new BMus curriculum in the post-Conservatorium model School of Music at the Australian National University. The design of such a programme raised many initial questions: in a research-led teaching environment – and in what is essentially a non-discipline - which research is prioritised? From where does the underpinning theory derive? Is 'Music & Digital Media' a creative practice course? How are the legal, virtual, business, philosophical, educational and media theories balanced across a 13-week semester? Following significant research into multi and interdisciplinary topics, a course design framework was established. Class content was supported and complemented with corresponding weekly activities and further study materials. 2 assessments – an individually negotiated written project and a group Podcast - were scheduled into the course, both taking student-led pedagogical approaches. A diverse range of learning contexts was also employed, including lecture, lab setting, seminar, workshop, forum, tutorial, Wiki discussion and Q&A models. A rigorous, local course committee was established allowing for essential feedback/ feed forward communication. This paper recognises both the advantages and challenges associated with what can be construed as 'imaginary', interdisciplinary topics. In this paper, issues of cohort expectation, research alignment, discipline priority and learning context are critically evaluated.

- 1. See programme page: http://www.law.harvard.edu/academics/curriculum/catalog/index.html?o=64792
- 2. Such as: The 'Music Matters' campaign led by the British Phonographic Industry [BPI], the 'Music Rules!' educational campaign led by the Recording Industry Association of America [RIAA] and the 'Internet File Sharing' resources available from the Australian Recording Industry Association [ARIA]
- 3. See program page: http://www.newcastle.edu.au/course/MTEC6705

KEYWORDS

Music, Digital, Media

AIMS

- Contextualise 'Music and Digital Media' in a post-Conservatorium music school;
- Design, execute and reflect upon a BMus course delivery featuring an emergent and indefinable topic;
- Underpin the aforementioned course with as diverse range of current, relevant research;
- Deliver the aforementioned course in a variety of situational contexts including lecture, tutorial, forum, lab, seminar and workshop styles, recognising both the theoretical and practical relevance of the topic;
- Complement face-to-face delivery mechanisms with structured ILE content and activities;
- Engage students in relevant theoretical and practical assessments; and
- Develop a rigorous student feedback and feed forward procedure surrounding both course content and assessments.

METHODS

A mixed methodology was used to carry out this research project. Firstly, iterative content and pedagogical analysis was undertaken on existing undergraduate courses/ modules entitled 'Music & Digital Media'. Secondly, the primary findings were cross-referenced with research in secondary sources from a range of multi-disciplinary angles including Law, Philosophy, Business, Music, Musicology, Media and Communications and Psychology. Thirdly, the author took notes following each 'Music & Digital Media' class and tutorial during Semester 2 2013 in order to amass a reflective journal. Finally, a process of critical reflection was undertaken following the course completion and submission of 'Student Evaluation of Learning & Teaching' [SELT] questionnaires.

OUTCOMES

Outcomes & Implications - Music & Digital Media is an interdisciplinary topic requiring a broad scope of theoretical underpinning from a range of disciplines; - Individual expectations of a course entitled 'Music & Digital Media' varied significantly; - BMus students were challenged by interdisciplinarity, particularly scientific fundamentals of digital audio, coding and audio compression for online media; - Content thematics require constant updating each year, particularly social networking, crowd funding and streaming; - Benefits to vague, interdisciplinary courses such as 'Music & Digital Media' include: allowing for a diverse range of student-led projects, potential to cover most/ all areas of interest; flexibility in content, delivery mechanism and assessment; - Challenges include: managing cohort and individual expectations; under/ over estimating practical group work capabilities; access to adequate lab and multi media resources, gathering reliable, cohort-wide feedback.

REFERENCES

Boehm, C. (2007) The Discipline That Never Was: Current Developments in Music Technology in Higher Education in Britain. *Journal of Music, Technology & Education*, 1(1), 7-21.

Burnard, P. (2014) (Ed.) *Developing Creativities in Higher Music Education: International Perspectives and Practices*. Oxon: Routledge

Palfrey, J. & Gasser, U. (2010). *Born digital: Understanding the first generation of digital natives*. New York: Basic Books.

"The Traveler Sonnet": The technology as a key element in the study of musical heritage through an inter-university and interdisciplinary educational experience

▍ Noemy Berbel-Gómez

    University of the Balearic Islands, Spain

▍ Alberto Cabedo-Mas

    University Jaume I of Castellón, Spain

▍ María Elena Riaño-Galán

    University of Cantabria, Spain

▍ Cristina Arriaga-Sanz

    University of the Basque Country, Spain

▍ Maravillas Díaz-Gómez

    University of the Basque Country, Spain

Abstract

During the first term of the academic year 2013-2014, we carried out an inter-university and interdisciplinary educational experience in four Spanish universities with students of the Bachelor's Degree in Early Childhood Education and the Bachelor's Degree in Primary Education. The activity, entitled "The Traveler Sonnet", was intended to increase students' knowledge on the traditional culture of different Spanish regions through an interdisciplinary and creative work that involved the areas of music, literature, visual arts and technology. Using virtual platforms and networks, students from each university worked collaboratively and cooperatively. Technology became an indispensable tool in the implementation and coordination of the experience. The common work made in these universities has promoted students' knowledge on cultural heritage and has also been a source of exchange and enrichment for both students and the teachers involved in these universities.

KEYWORDS

technology, inter-university experience, traditional heritage

AIMS

The aim of this paper is to present an inter-university and interdisciplinary experience using technological resources as a tool for coordination between different Spanish universities and as a platform for presentation of visual and sonic products carried out. The Traveler Sonnet is intended to increase knowledge on heritage through the study of traditional culture in four Spanish regions through the creation of literary production – sonnets –, musical compositions, illustrations, audiovisual montages and public performances. It therefore upholds the use of musical heritage as an educational resource within the classroom (Riaño-Galán & Cabedo-Mas, 2013). The objective is to promote creativity and innovation, using technology as a tool for the implementation of key competences in the initial training for teachers (Giráldez, 2013).

METHODS

This interdisciplinary experience coordinated the areas of literature, fine art, music and technology in four Spanish universities: University of the Basque Country, University of Cantabria, University Jaume I of Castellón and University of the Balearic Islands. In total, 11 teachers and 412 students participated in the activities involved. Both students and teachers worked cooperatively using virtual platforms, which allowed them to share ideas, to show their work and to carry out different tasks together. The following guidelines were executed in each university to develop common procedures. First, students were distributed in small working groups which cooperatively wrote a sonnet – 14-line poem – dealing with one of ten themes that had been previously stated. The sonnets had to be inspired by students' traditional culture; each topic therefore included, in the end, sonnets evoking the cultural heritage from four Spanish regions – Basque Country, Cantabria, Valencian Community and the Balearic Islands. Second, students composed music and created a sonic environment to each sonnet. All sounds were expected to be inspired by one traditional song chosen from the musical heritage of each region. In parallel, they conducted a visual and plastic work to take and manipulate images and videos dealing with the sonnet's topic. One of the key lines of the process entailed understanding technology as a resource to enhance musical experience (Webster, 2002). Finally, students performed an audiovisual presentation of the ten sonnets, one for each theme, set with the music, pictures and videos they had shaped. The process of audiovisual creation consisted of scripting, digitizing images, video recording, speech recording and audiovisuals montage. The coordination between the teachers involved in the different universities was essential for the precise execution of the experience through the design and sequencing of activities, processes and results. A wiki tool was used to connect and communicate both teachers and students. The teachers from each university designed together and provided the materials that enabled students to develop the projects and tasks. The students from different universities who approached the same topic, had to work together to design and build the creative products. Throughout the process, the students shared gradually the work they had made through this very wiki, allowing colleagues from other universities to collaborate and continue with the activities and performances. Concerning the evaluation of the Traveler Sonnet, organizational and coordination elements were taking into account, together with the quality of the creative products, assessed by both teachers and students – text, music, photograph and audiovisual material, performance. Students' needs and degree of satisfaction were also considered. Questionnaires, learning portfolios and self-criticism of the work and the process done were included among the assessment techniques used.

Outcomes

The results of the Traveler Sonnet included all the audiovisual materials made by the students. They were all posted in the virtual space of the wiki. A montage of ten videos, one for each stated theme, brought together the work from different working groups in different universities. Once the visual and sonic activity was completed, a public performance, containing and an exhibition of the audiovisual material produced, was carried out. Regarding the evaluation of the inter-university experience, we emphasize that it enhanced the acquisition of basic and transversal competences, the creativity and the ability to successfully approach teamwork. It also improved the knowledge on the cultural heritage of different Spanish regions through traditional songs, rituals, dances, and other cultural features. Furthermore, it enabled the use of ICT tools in teaching and learning methodologies, in the development and coordination of students and teachers work, and as a tool for inter-university communication.

DISCUSSION

The students involved in the Traveler Sonnet have deepened and reflected on the relevance of the interconnection between theory and practice in the learning process, the importance of the autonomy and the self-learning in music education and the interrelations in collaborative learning. After the public performance, the students reported to experience feelings in relation to personal and group commitment, the satisfaction of achieving goals and the respect for the work made by themselves and their colleagues. Finally, this artistic work helped students to increase knowledge on their own cultural heritage and on the cultural traditions and products of different regions of Spain and to value the use of technology within a creative process. Pre-service teachers in early childhood and primary education not only acquire knowledge from their teachers, but also from habits and ways of working. Thence, we consider that participating in an interdisciplinary and inter-university experience enabled students to confirm the benefits of collaborative learning in all the subjects involved.

ACKNOWLEDGEMENTS

The authors acknowledge the Ministry of Economy and Compet Ministry of Economy and Competitiveness for the funding of the Project *"Música, danza y ritual en el encuentro iberoamericano. El patrimonio compartido y su trascendencia en la educación"* [Music, dance and ritual in the Ibero-American encounter. The shared heritage and its importance in education], HAR2011-30164-C03-03. This work derives from it.

REFERENCES

Giráldez Hayes, A. (2013). Enseñar artes en un mundo digital: Diez propuestas para la formación del professorado. PÓS: Revista do Programa de Pós-graduação em Artes da Escola de Belas Artes da UFMG, 3(5), 85-104.

Riaño-Galán, M.E., & Cabedo-Mas, A. (2013). La importancia del patrimonio musical en el aula: Estudio sobre la opinión del profesorado en educación infantil. Eufonía: Didáctica de la música, 58, 67-78.

Webster, P. (2002). Computer-based technology and music teaching and learning. In R. Colwell & C. Richardson (Eds). The New Handbook of Research on Music Teaching and

Learning (pp. 416-439). New York: Oxford University Press.

A brittle discipline: Music Technology and Third Culture Thinking

|| Carola Boehm

Contemporary Arts, Manchester Metropolitan University, UK

ABSTRACT

Five years ago I wrote an introductory article for a journal, in which I considered the state of music technology degrees in our universities in the UK. Having seen where higher education (HE) policy has taken us, and having had the fortunate opportunity to be heavily involved in shaping genuinely interdisciplinary provision that considers interdisciplinarity with all its warts and perks , I thought it time to consider the implications of HE policy on interdisciplinary subject areas, to explore specifically the gaps that I identified five years ago and to consider how the current climate is affecting them. This article will cover the ever-widening disciplinary gaps that are appearing in HE and focuses specifically on those gaps that are substantially affecting various interdisciplinary areas of learning and research in HE. It uses music technology as an example case study. Even the process of placing of this article into an academic journal demonstrates the existing challenges; in its interdisciplinary nature its eligibility to feature in a subject-specific periodical might be questioned despite its high relevance for it. The article also attempts to demonstrate models that support interdisciplinary teaching and research, which hopefully are able to mind and furthermore mend various existent gaps. With any luck it will disrupt some of our pre-postmodern concepts of what a university is, to be superseded by a more postmodern acceptance of society as constructivist learning communities, and universities as enablers of these communities. In this exploration, I follow a trajectory, from exploring to mending the gaps, and then finally to discussing in detail a specific methodology that represents one way forward out of the interdisciplinary quagmire.

Keywords

music technology, interdisciplinarity, practice as research

Aims

The article aimes to expose the implications of HE policy on interdisciplinary subject areas, to explore specifically the gaps that were identified five years ago and to consider how the current climate is affecting these. It attempts to demonstrate models that support interdisciplinary teaching and research, which hopefully are able to mind and furthermore mend various existent gaps. With any luck it will disrupt some of our pre-postmodern concepts of what a university is, to be superseded by a more postmodern acceptance of society as constructivist learning communities, and universities as enablers of these communities.

Methods

Discursive exploration of a complex issue influenced by external educational policies.

Outcomes

- Establish and make explicit models for interdisciplinary learning and research, with focus on its relevance for the area of music technology.
- Raise awareness for policy makers and educationalists.
- To have minded the gaps.

Conclusion

The British HE sector is known to live in a constant climate of change. For better or for worse, there is no other country in Europe which has had more governmental policy changes imposed on universities than the UK. It has had to adapt, grow, shrink, change and shift every time a significant change in policy was introduced. Of course this might be the result of the UK political adversarial two-party system supported by first-past-the post voting and it is interesting to note that those HE sectors that are considered more stable are in countries where more representative voting systems are utilised with more incremental policy development. But UK Universities have always stepped up to the challenge, with only some smaller institutions stumbling along the way. The sector is amazingly resilient, and I for one feel that it still demonstrates the value that universities hold for society as a whole. As advocated in this article, I believe that the biggest challenges we face today are of an interdisciplinary nature, and although our research cultures have easily adapted to this (with some slower but nevertheless steady progress in the structures of funding research), we are challenged by our undergraduate learning provisions which still have disciplinary cultures in place that stem from the last century. They mirror what happens in secondary education, and it is here that more courageous attempts to break the disciplinary divides need to happen. Music technology itself, in all its guises, is flourishing as ever. It has become a part of the educational establishment and, as a subject, a pillar of our economic wealth. That a subject area such as this should have a hard time establishing itself as a discipline (there is no such thing as a music technologist) has rather to do with university structures and the nature of disciplines as social constructs. I, for one, have somehow come to the conclusion that in the case of music technology, it does not matter what part of which area is taught where, whether electro-acoustic/sonic composition is taught only in music departments, music informatics only in computer science departments, or sound engineering predominantly in music colleges. What matters more is that HE institutions and research cultures have to adopt a more open stance towards methodological choices, that researchers need to be taught the cultures and histories of disciplinary divides to free them and give them confidence to chose methodologies that are appropriate to the enquiry, and that these "would emerge in the course of the inquiry rather than be predetermined in the form of discipline-bound theories, methods, and schools of thought" (Mourad 1997) .

REFERENCES

Boehm, C. (2007). The discipline that never was. *Journal for Music, Technology and Education.* Vol 1 No. 1.

Collini, S. (2010). Browne's Gamble. *London Review of Books.* Vol. 32 No. 21, pp. 23-25.

Linden, J. (2012). *The Monster in our Midst: The Materialisation of Practice as Research in the British Academy.* PhD, Manchester Metropolitan University.

Researching coding collaboratively in classrooms: Developing Sonic Pi

▌ Pamela Burnard
   University of Cambridge, Faculty of Education, UK

▌ Samuel Aaron
   University of Cambridge, Computer Laboratory, UK

▌ Alan F. Blackwell
   University of Cambridge, Computer Laboratory, UK

ABSTRACT

Live coding is a growing international phenomenon that brings together the creative skills of musicking and computer programming; a mode of digital creativity that considers coding as a performance. Live coding introduces the exciting notion of 'liveness' with composition and improvisation happening in the immediacy of performance. Coding exists as a much higher sonic abstraction than that of standard Western music notation; it affords the performer the ability to compose in the immediate or real time of improvised performance, thus merging improvisation, composition and performance creativities. Sonic Pi is a new open source software tool and platform for the Raspberry Pi computer, designed to enable school children to learn programming by creating music. (The Raspberry Pi charitable foundation delivers low cost computing technology to a large audience of over 1 million young people and creative enthusiasts.) In this presentation we share insights from a recent research project which develops new practices to enable, empower, inform and inspire students to engage in opportunities to create digital music and new digital creativities in music. The presentation responds to technology disruption and subcultural music practices (e.g breakbeat and dubstep) by involving musicians as educators and computer scientists as musicians to enable young people to engage creatively with a digital instrument that is accessible and can be used to provide new forms of performance. This provides ways of working that open up new educational and business models and modalities for creating new digital creativities. Despite the possibilities that digital technologies are acknowledged to offer music education, the incorporation of new technological practices into music curricula remains a challenging political, social and practical task. In many cases 'school music' practices are presented in an abstract manner that is removed from everyday experience. Because of this they can lack the authenticity of engagement. This paper will address these issues as chosen points of reference and will examine ways in which schools can be innovative spaces for nurturing new collaborative learning digital communities. In terms of connecting research and practices in the field of music education, it will give illustrations of: the pedagogies and creativities developed as a result of this kind of work; and the creative ways in which coding can promote cultural, scientific and artistic exchange, and be a catalyst for change. "Acknowledgements" The project and research featured in this paper was funded by the Raspberry Pi Foundation.

KEYWORDS

Coding, Digital learning, Partnerships

AIMS

The aims of the study were: (i) to document how coding pedagogies were developed collaboratively between the computer scientist and IT teacher and (ii) to understand how secondary school students engaged in and made sense of learning to code and create digital music using Sonic Pi, an new open source software tool and platform for the Raspberry Pi computer use in formal education contexts.

METHODS

The study was carried out with 2 secondary school IT classes, the computer scientist who developed Sonic Pi and the IT teacher who was also a music enthusiast. Research methods included (i) in-depth interviews, (ii) stimulated recall and meaning oriented reflection tasks, and (iii) text-based graphical programming scripts as expressions of the creative and learning processes.

OUTCOMES

Findings presented will address two key outcomes which concern (i) how students perceive engagement with learning to code and engage creatively with digital instruments as tools for programming their own new music and (ii) how new pedagogic practices are necessary for effective learning.

CREATING CHANGE IN DIGITAL LEARNING COMMUNITIES: THE POWER OF PARTNERSHIPS

The need to radically change how schools see their futures and the restructuring of teacher/learner relationships, along with teacher/computer scientists will be argued. Schools need to see themselves as organisations that are in the vanguard of coming to terms with and being centres of new digital learning communities and creativities. Schools need to place a high priority on and promote digital learning communities engagement. Promoting digital learning engagement is vital to innovation and to the creation of new pedagogies, partnerships and learning about learning.

ACKNOWLEDGEMENTS

The project and research featured in this paper was funded by the Raspberry Pi Foundation.

REFERENCES

Aaron, S. and Blackwell, Al (2013) From Sonic Pi to Overtone: Creative musical experiences with domain specific and functional languages. *ACM Digital Library*. Boston, USA.

Finney, J. and Burnard, P. (2009) (Eds.) *Music Education with Digital Technology*. London: Continuum.

Burnard, P. (2012) *Musical Creativities in Practice*. Oxford: OUP.

Children's compositional strategies in their interaction with digital tools: a micro-genetic analytical approach

| Vasiliki Charisi

Institute of Education, University of London, UK

Abstract

This paper aims to investigate young children's development of musical thinking in the context of music making, which is supported by digital tools. In this context, music composition will be considered as a process - which arises through multiple interactions - rather, than as a final product or achievement. Although a big picture has started to be shaped for the depiction of those processes for adult composers and children, a need for their investigation in a micro-level has arisen. Data that are presented in this paper were collected by observations of 16 children who were called to create musical pieces with the support of digital tools, within 6 weakly sessions. A micro-genetic analytical approach of their verbal and non-verbal interactions revealed patterns regarding children's compositional strategies, which differ (i) in time of appearance, (ii) in frequency and (iii) in the ways of transition from one strategy to another.

Keywords

digital tools, compositional strategies, micro-genetic analysis

Aims

A considerable body of empirical and theoretical research has shed light to the compositional processes for adult composers and several models have been developed that depict those processes in various ways (Dave Collins & Dunn, 2011). At the same time, researchers with an interest in children's behaviours have investigated compositional processes in children's interactions with physical or digital environments, in primary and secondary education (Bamberger, 2011). Nevertheless, when the focus shifts towards young children's thinking processes in music making, it seems that there not exist adequate research, yet.

This paper will attempt to investigate young children's musical thinking by looking at the slight nuances 'between the stages'. In particular, the aim of this ongoing research is to describe the genesis of children's compositional strategies and their micro- development, within their music making, which is supported by digital tools. Aspects of theoretical studies about children's musical development are taken into consideration.

METHODS

Researchers have used a variety of methodological approaches in their attempt to investigate children's music making, which include post-hoc interviews, verbal protocol analysis, observations, and examination of children's musical products, among others. For the purposes of the present research, 16 children - 5 to 7 years old - were called to create musical pieces within the time of 6 sessions for about 30 minutes each, in the course of 2 months. Their music making was taken place in a naturalistic setting, in the computer laboratory of the school, with which children were familiar. Two different digital environments were chosen to facilitate children's music making; the first one was especially designed for children's compositional activities and the second one has been mainly used by adults for electroacoustic real-time music composition. A collaborative setting - 8 pairs of children - was considered as the most suitable setting for this research, in order to support children's verbalization of their thoughts. The researcher was present in all sessions, but she tried to have a minimal participation. All the sessions were videotaped and the musical material from whole process was collected in an audio and visual form.

For the purpose of this paper, children's dialogues and non-verbal behaviour were transcribed and analysed.

Initial qualitative analysis revealed 44 verbal and non-verbal behaviours, which were later organized in 25 keywords, which fall into 5 groups:

- Cognitive behaviours
- Social behaviours
- Emotional responses
- Interactions with the digital tools
- Researcher's interventions

Findings indicated the existence of patterns regarding the sequence of specific behaviours within the same participant over time and among participants, as well as interrelations of behaviours of the above-mentioned groups. Additionally, indications about the genesis and the development of children's cognitive strategies created the need for a further analysis in a micro-level.

A micro-genetic analytical approach (Siegler, 2006) was adopted to investigate the course of children's compositional strategies.

This present research fits all three criteria of this method of analysis, namely:

- Observations span a period of rapid change in competency;
- The density of observations is high relative to the rate of change; and
- The observations are subjected to an intensive, trial- by-trial analysis to infer the processes that give rise to change.

This micro-analytical approach will allow the examination of children's strategies regarding the changes that occur during their engagement with music making. In this paper only the path and the rate of the changes, as well as the mechanisms that cause the changes are presented.

OUTCOMES

Data analysis of this research is still ongoing. With a focus on children's cognitive behaviours, initial findings reveal that the same strategies appear in all children, which include:

- Spontaneous musicking;
- Sound exploration;
- Assessment;
- Reasoning;
- Deliberate musicking;
- Planning

However, different children vary (i) in the time that each of the above strategies appears, (ii) in the frequency of the same strategy as well as (iii) in the mechanisms that produce the transition from one strategy to another. Social interactions and emotional responses seemed to be related with the development of the strategies, but they were not constantly present. Cross-examination of the strategies revealed a partial overlapping among different strategies.

Discussion

Research on music making in early childhood has seen composition as a mainly investigative processes with improvisational characteristics. Nevertheless, digital technology for music making may provide additional affordances for the genesis and the development of a variety of strategies by young children for their musical creations. Looking at the microdevelopment of those strategies might help researchers and practitioners for a better understanding of young children's musical thinking and may contribute to the development of new pedagogies for music making in early childhood, which is supported by digital tools.

Acknowledgements

This article has been based on the author's ongoing PhD research at the Institute of Education, University of London. The author would like to take the opportunity to acknowledge the high level of continuous support and expert guidance provided by her supervisors Prof. G. Welch and Dr E. Himonides and to thank them. She would like also to thank the children for taking part in this research. This study has been financially supported by the Greek State Scholarships Foundation.

References

Bamberger, J. (2011). The collaborative invention of meaning: A short history of evolving ideas. *Psychology of Music*, 39(1), 82-101.

Collins, D., & Dunn, M. (2011). Problem-solving strategies and processes in musical composition: Observations in real time. *Journal of Music, Technology and Education*, 4(1), 47-76.

Siegler, R. S. (2006). Microgenetic Analyses of Learning. In D. Kuhn & R. S. Siegler (Eds.), *Handbook of Child Psychology (Vol. 2: Cognition, perception, and language*, pp. 464-510). Hoboken, NJ: Wiley.

Influence of sequencing software in musician competences

▌ Francisco José Cuadrado Méndez
 Universidad Loyola Andalucía, Spain

Abstract

The progressive development and implementation of new audio and music technologies, tools and resources have changed the entire concept of music composition, integrating recording processes into composition and improvisation. As Thèberge concludes, "songs are no simply composed, performed and then recorded. More and more, the studio becomes a compositional tool in its own right" (1997: 216). As a recent field study on composition techniques with adolescents has outcome, "participants' work often crossed through aspects of pre-production, production, and post-production in an overlapping manner, making it difficult and at times inappropriate to use these overarching categories to organize their creative processes" (Tobias, 2013: 218). The evolution of musical sequencing, recording, editing and mixing software, and the implementation of new tools and capabilities in the so called workstations have had an impact over the knowledge and competencies that the musician needs to acquire in its work.

Keywords

Sequencing software, Music creation, Creativity

Aims

The aim of our study has been to analyse the influence that new tools, functions and resources in popular sequencing software have over the composition process and over the skills, knowledge and competences that the musician needs to acquire.

Methods

Two methods have been combined in this study. The first one has been the analysis of the different resources of one of the most used software sequencers. Its functions and tools have been evaluated from the perspective of the improvements they may introduce into the composition process, the hypothetical changes in the workflow and the new skills that are needed to be acquired.

The second research method employed has been a field study among musicians that use these tools. With the result of the sequencer analysis as a starting point, a specific questionnaire has been designed, divided in several sections, to evaluate their use of these new tools, their composition workflow and the Influence of the sequencer in the development as a musician.

The questionnaire has been distributed through an online platform, open during two weeks. The call for participants has been disseminated on three of the biggest online communities of musicians: Hispasonic (Spanish language community, with more than 350.000 users), Steinberg forum: official English forum for Cubase, with more than 40.000 registered users, and Sound on sound: online magazine specialized on music and technology.

220 valid questionnaires have been submitted, by participants from 38 different countries. The average age is between 21 and 35 years old. The main activity of the participants is composer (42%), followed by music producer (30%) and sound engineer (about 15%). Musical styles with more presence have been Pop, Rock and Electronic (between 40 and 60% users), followed by classical, popular, jazz and music for audiovisual and stage productions (between 26 and 32% users).

Outcomes

As the result of the analysis, a number of tools and resources have been selected and organised in three main categories: composing, sound modelling and production. The different tools and resources have been evaluated according to: the ease of use (number of steps needed to obtain results or similarities with other previous known tools), the technical knowledge needed to use it (understanding it as non musical knowledge, but one related to computer use or sound engineering processes), and the level of the improvement hypothetically supposed. Comparing the analysis with the results of the field study, the study has evidenced that there are certain tools that have been fully incorporated into the composition process, while others are practically not used, or its use relay on different factors. The use of the sequencer has also clear positive effects on musicians and their creative process. Finally, the field research has helped to define and characterize different kind of workflows in the composition process.

ACKNOWLEDGEMENTS

Sound on sound, Steinberg, PSP Audioware

REFERENCES

Tobias, E.S. (2013). Composing, songwriting, and producing: Informing popular music pedagogy. *Research Studies in Music Education, 35,* p. 213.

Gilreath, P. (2006). *The guide to MIDI orchestration.* MusicWorks Atlanta.

Fouce, H. (2010). *Tecnologías y medios de comunicación en la era digital* Revista Comunicar, 34, 65-72.

Roca, F. (2004): *Creatividad y Comunicación Musical desde las Nuevas Tecnologías* Revista Comunicar, 23, 31-36.

Théberge, P. (1997). *Any sound you can imagine: Making music/consuming technology.* Middletown, CT: Wesleyan University Press.

Preparing the music technology toolbox: addressing the education-industry dilemma

▌ Robert Davis
    Leeds Metropolitan University, UK

▌ Steven Parker
    Leeds Metropolitan University, UK

▌ Paul Thompson
    Leeds Metropolitan University, UK

Abstract

The growth in popularity of music technology degree programs in the UK has been paralleled by the apparent decline of informal apprenticeship systems that have typically provided a gateway to employment in the recording industry. This paper takes a critical approach to the tensions that exist between higher education and the music industries by exploring contemporary and historical approaches of apprenticeship. Drawing on interviews with industry professionals, current students and recent graduates who have achieved some success in the music industries, this paper explores some of the perceptions, myths and contradictions of the apprenticeship-training model with changes in the contemporary professional environment.

Our findings suggest that training for the music industries is more flexible and open-ended than some of the published narratives on apprenticeship would suggest. In addition, educational frameworks over the past 20 years have often focused on the technical aspects of studio practice at the expense of the social, aesthetic and human skills required by the industry. These formal frameworks often only focus on the transference of knowledge to the individual (Thompson and McIntyre, 2013) diminishing or ignoring the important processes of interaction with the participants in the field.

Using the metaphor of a professional 'toolbox', we argue there is a need for an approach that reconsiders the industry-education divide and considers the value of the educational process in a much wider, contemporary framework. Some 20 years since the initial development of Music Technology programmes in the UK, and in the context of the rapidly changing nature of the music industries, it is an appropriate time to reconsider the nature and relevance of music technology programmes in higher education.

KEYWORDS

apprentices, graduates, industry-ready

AIMS

This paper discusses the tensions that exist between higher education and the need to produce industry-ready students by examining a number of initiatives undertaken at Leeds Metropolitan University.

CONTEXTUAL CONSIDERATIONS

The growth in popular music degree programmes in the UK has been well documented most notably by Boehm (2006) who indicated that the name Music Technology was linked to 351 degrees distributed over some 62 institutions. One of the key ideas to emerge from her discussion was the notion that these degrees were strongly interdisciplinary and viewed as highly vocational.

The rise in these courses during the 1990s and beyond can be understood as the confluence of several important factors including the availability of affordable music technology centred around the computer; the expansion of numbers in higher education as part of the then Labour government's agenda of creating 'knowledge driven economy' (DTI/CEPR, 1999) and an emerging recognition of the economic importance of what have now become known as the 'creative industries'. As Pamela Burnard notes in her discussion of Musical Creativities:

There has been much debate in recent decades, although nothing approaching a consensus, about the concept of musical creativity. This debate has intensified as governments have pressurized the creative and cultural industries and other social institutions, particularly those involved with education, to articulate what constitutes the value of creativity, whether in terms of communication, or in relation to the global economy. Governments and industries are not only telling artists and educations what they should do but also prescribing the terms in which they should think and the ideals towards which they should aspire in their creativity practices. (Burnard: 2012, 7).

For those establishing courses in Music Technology in the 1990s, government sponsored documents such as the National Advisory Committee on Creative and Cultural Education's report *All Our Futures: Creativity, Culture and Education* and the Creative *Industries Mapping Document* (Smith *et al.*, 1998) provided an important cornerstone in the legitimisation of this hybrid discipline. At the same time, the promise of a creative and cultural economy, of producing industry-ready graduates and of providing entry into the new knowledge driven economy was disappointing in comparison to the rhetoric of the time. According to '*A Manifesto for the Creative Economy*'. (Nesta: 2013).

Evidence suggests that most universities haven't been producing the kind of talent that the creative industries demand. We see this in the poor employment outcomes of graduates from creative media specialist degrees evidenced in *Next Gen* (only 12 per cent of those graduating from games courses secured employment in the industry within six months of leaving university) and other studies. (Bakhshi et al. 2013, p. 103).

The tensions between industry and education suggested by these reports do, on the whole, take a reductive view of employment' and overlooks the multifarious and multifaceted nature of the creative industry. Such a point was made in the critical study of Williamson and Cloonan who concluded that:

> ...there is no such thing as a single music industry. There are, however, people working in a range of industries centred around music. These are music industries and it them that we should study and engage with'. (Williamson, Cloonan. 2007, 320).

By placing our study in the wider perspective of the music industries we aim to re-examine the industry-education intersection from a number of perspectives in order to re-examine what appear to be competing voices in what David Ashton (2010) refers to as the 'industry-ready agenda'. As the politics of austerity intensify and further impacts on this agenda, we find this an appropriate time to pause and reflect on the nature of our courses and their purpose.

The relevance of this topic has become more focused not only with the significant increase in student fees, but also with the creation of a £15m fund to support the creation of traineeships, apprenticeships and paid internships in post-16 education. The title of this scheme is 'The Creative Employment Programme'. With headlines such as 'creating 6500 jobs in 1000 days' and statements such as 'The creative economy looks buoyant in comparison to the UK economy as a whole. News statistics from the DCMS outline that employment growth stood at 6% in the creative economy between 2011 and 2012, in comparison to just 0.7% in the wider economy' (Mitchell, 2014), we see a continuation and intensification the line of thinking that the creative economy serves economic and employment ends.

Our focus is largely on the apprenticeship-training model, which has played an important part in the development of industry-ready workforce long before music technology became a subject for study in higher education. Our longer-term goal is to re-examine both our undergraduate and post-graduate provision with a view to finding a sustainable way to address the industry-education dilemma.

METHODOLOGY AND RESEARCH

In order to explore the perceptions, experiences and contradictions of the apprenticeship-training model in the music industries, we adopted a broadly ethnographic approach in the understanding that ethnography 'increases our knowledge of the details of cultural processes and practices' (Cohen. 1993,135). Moreover, we began our exploration with the gathering of evidence from a broad range of participants, varying in age, gender and involvement in the recording industries. They were selected in an attempt to reflect the spectrum of individual experiences across a number of generations and geographical areas. Participants ranged from established recording engineers and record producers to recent graduates who are now employed in the recording industries. The primary method used was interview in order to, as Thomas Lindlof explains,

...understand their perspective on a scene, to retrieve experiences from the past, to gain expert insight or information, to obtain descriptions of events or scenes that are normally unavailable for observation, to foster trust, to understand a sensitive or intimate relationship, or to analyse certain kinds of discourse. (Lindlof. 1995, 5).

Questions during the interviews were designed to explore specific topics such as musical and industry background, motivation, preparation for work, entry to employment, changes in the industries and thoughts on formal education in this area. By examining the profession prior to the expansion of music technology courses in the 1990s, the paper provides a comparative viewpoint to examine current trends in formal educational programmes and courses.

Interviews were conducted over a three-year period from September 2011 to March 2014 and were loosely directed by a series of fifteen questions. This further helped the responses to be appropriately grouped by topic and identify common themes and trends. The interviews, transcribed from either video or audio recordings, further provided a useful platform for comparison between participants and drawing related themes from the data. The interviews were complemented through participant-observation of professionals, students and apprenticeships contributing to industry-ready initiatives and working alongside practitioners in the recording studio environment. For the purposes of disseminating the findings from the study, the participants have either retained their anonymity or assumed a pseudonym.

FINDINGS

Industry Perspectives

Interviews with ten professionals working in the music industry along with reflections from one of the authors of this paper, provided a way of capturing aspects of both formal and informal apprenticeships that offered a route into the recording and associated music industries such as post production for film or TV. A good deal of the early experiences of these professionals relied o   n what Jewson refers to as 'peripheral participation and situated learning' (2007: 156). In this way, learning goes beyond achieving a formalised set of learning outcomes and moves towards a more diverse experience where learning occurs. This is due, in part, to the lack of any formalised training in apprenticeship and was evident in all of the responses from participants who had begun their career in larger recording facilities:

There was no formal training it was "dive straight in" and one of the earliest lessons I learnt from that, which is a very important credo that I still hold today was to not pretend you know something when you don't. If someone asks you and you don't know how to do it, just say "I'm sorry, I don't know". I still do that now.

This apparent lack of a formal structure meant that designated tasks, roles and responsibilities were staggered over a longer period of time in which certain roles or tasks had to be performed and mastered before one moved onto others:

Probably for those first couple of months, as a tea boy/runner, I was probably 9 to 5 office hours just to see was I reliable, capable of getting the tea, getting the sandwiches, getting the coffee machine going every morning and doing

> whatever else was asked. By three months it was decided that I could be left on a session.

However, one engineer highlighted a particular issue with performing tasks within the hierarchy of the recording studio:

> The problem is the one thing that you can't really do as a tape-op/runner is ask questions; you're supposed to be kind of invisible…so you observe, you watch what people are doing but there's no one really there to show you.

This process did have significant advantages too as it allowed participants to become more involved as their skills and knowledge developed over time. A number of the participants noted that it took several years (ranging from 2 to 6 years) to progress from their starting position as a runner to assisting on a session.

Evident in all of the responses were the expectations of technical knowledge and skills and one engineer noted that:

> You're expected to know it [the studio equipment] inside out and you have to learn that pretty quickly so I'd spend a fair bit of time looking through manuals but in down time I'd be there really trying to learn, rather than messing about with compressors and settings I'd be sat with the RADAR making sure I could do what people would ask me to do. You know, "can you cut this from here to here" and it was the same with tape editing, I sat there with a few old reels that were kicking around, added a bit of music to them from a CD and I'd sit there actually cutting old tape and trying to figure out how it works.

Another producer explained that:

> I've always been fascinated with electronics and audio equipment and that's helped me to think in terms of wires, cables and signal flow rather than anything else. But when you get used to thinking like that then it's learning to try and throw that away so it becomes almost second nature to you and you don't have to think about all the equipment and everything because you want that aspect to become more transparent so you can get to real reason why a band come to a studio, which is to make a record.

The overwhelming majority of participants in the study spent more than 12 hours a day in their role as part of their working day and this sizeable amount of time spent in the studio, particularly in the early stages of development in their career, meant that situated learning occurred through observation and interaction with other members of the field including musicians, producers, record company representatives and other engineers. One engineer explained that observing in the studio as part of his assisting role enabled him to learn the process of making decisions:

> *I was lucky enough to work at the tail end of the analogue thing and to work with some people who didn't know anything else and that is all about decision-making; dropping in and no comp'ing.... decision making on the spot and I do a lot of that as well, I hate leaving anything. I feel the best people work through instinct and after a period of time you know how to make those types of decisions and that is something that you watch people do. The longer you spend in watching people making decisions that you really learn to hear inside music, your ear becomes naturally critical...In the same way that a Navy admiral would make instant decisions with an educated and experienced insight, it's the same thing with making records but you learn that from just spending a lot of time with people.*

One professional explained that:

> *The longer you spend in watching people making decisions that you really learn to hear inside music, your ear becomes naturally critical...In the same way that a Navy admiral would make instant decisions with an educated and experienced insight, it's the same thing with making records but you learn that from just spending a lot of time with people.*

From this particular viewpoint, situated learning and participating in the professional atmosphere of the studio provided something more than being peer-critical which, of course, lacks the benefit of working with experienced professionals. As Thompson and McIntyre (2013) have noted, interaction between the individual and the field is an important aspect of becoming creative in a particular domain. In the 1970s one interviewee recalled in the studio 'there was that chance...' not only to participate but to meet musicians and learn from them. Learning from others in the recording studio also highlighted the social practices of recording and all of the participants emphasised the importance of learning the social aspects of recording in the studio: social skills become extremely important.

Absent, from these interviews are those apprentices who did not complete their time and who left the industry. Little is said about these people, which allows us to reflect on the qualities of the people who did remain. In general terms, however, Unwin's study of apprenticeships (2007) in other sectors, suggests that while 'just over 50 per cent of apprentices achieve the prescribed qualifications, in some service sectors, achievement rates are staggeringly low: for example, 16 per cent in health and social care, 31 per cent in hospitality' (2007: 118).

Student Perspectives

Over the past two years, Leeds Metropolitan University, like other institutions, has organised an industry experience where visiting artists work with students on a defined project. During this time, students take a number of roles in the studio. This differs from everyday experiences because it is a sustained programme over a number of days rather than hourly sessions over a number of weeks. This experience provided an opportunity for discussion and initial reflections on the experience and skills required of this work. A number of key ideas emerged from the discussion. These comments have been extracted from the discussion because they specifically addressed elements which were not part of the curricular experience of their course:

> *I think [the most important skill] was people skills, pure people skills... you had to get to know someone quite quickly.... and you needed to have a relationship with the person you are working with... it makes it much more comfortable, a much more enjoyable place to work.*

Additionally, as well as relationships developed over the week, it was understood that:

> *...you have to keep the flow of the sessions.....when we do modules at uni, the flow doesn't necessarily matter....you are normally recording yourself or your friend so you just get on with it.*

In the course of the discussion, one student returned to this subject:

> *Going back to the whole flow thing...you can physically feel when you're slowing the process and you're losing something in that and it was more a thing of not wanting to cause that but to facilitate the process as much as you could.*

Also participating in this conversation were two former students who are now working professionally in post-production in London. They discussed flow in professional sessions in terms of 'steering' the client in order to ensure that there was flow and that the task is completed on time. Thinking back to their own experience of student projects on the course, one ex-student noted that this issue of flow and working with clients was something that they learned once they had entered the industry: working alongside peers in the studio had not prepared them for that aspect of their work.

Our recently qualified graduates were also responsible for training graduate entrants in their studios. From their comments it would appear that, in their words:

> *a lot of [graduates] don't know how studios work...especially the work flow. We're developing a training programme...because we have found that people are not coming in with the technical base [required].*

It would be safe to say that any graduate entrant to any profession would require a period of study to assimilate the everyday working process of the profession. However, it raises an interesting perspective of preparing the industry-ready student. When students were asked directly about their response to the industry week one third year student stated:

> *We learned more in the employability fortnight than we had learned on the course so far...even if it was only a simulated working environment, that sense of it was hugely important I think.*

Reflecting on this comment, another student noted that:

> *you can spend hours and hours learning how to use microphones [and] compression...it means nothing until you are in with someone working on a genuine product, that's what it is all about, this is what we are aiming for, and we're only just now [in our final year] touching on it...having that real world experience teaches you a great deal about yourself as well.*

A rough and ready calculation suggests that on a three year programme at university, a student might be expected to access the studio for around 500 hours. In the same period, a busy professional might work around 7500 hours and based on a 40 hour week, someone on the new government-sponsored apprenticeship programme, could achieve around 5760 hours. In terms of real-world and industry-ready experiences, these differences are significant.

Industry Perspectives on formal education

Although there are related aspects of learning in both formal and informal situations, a number of participants rightfully emphasised the differences in apprenticeship and formal education programmes, as one Producer who has worked in the UK and the USA over a 30-year career explains:

> *You can't make a valid comparison between apprenticeships and formal education because they serve different purposes. On the educational end it's geared towards the end result of the piece of paper you get, or specific goals in this module or that project. If you're in a real-time studio situation you're talking about being in a commercial environment and everything that goes along with that ... you know from making the tea to cleaning up after they've left and that whole sort of client relationship that you can't put into practice in an educational environment.*

One engineer explains further that:

> *From HE there's that element of observation that's missing, observing tons of different practitioners on a daily basis you just can't beat that as a form of education and it's so difficult to replicate a real scenario.*

Another recording engineer supports this view:

> *The advantage we had was that we saw things that didn't work and we were able to fill up our toolbox with these experiences.*

Therefore In order to include aspects of a real environment one Nashville-based Record Producer suggests that:

> *They [Educational Institutions] should offer classes in all the things that could go wrong with a session. You've got a high-dollar client in and the first day he's in the hospital with a drug overdose, what do you do? Are you going to get paid? Is the studio going to get paid? You're in the middle of a session and the pro-tools computer dies but you've got a tape machine, what's going to happen? Are you going to continue to record?*

Furthermore, a number of industry participants emphasized the view that they were still learning, still filling their 'toolbox' through experience:

> *You don't really learn to drive until you've actually passed your test...you don't really start to learn until you're doing it for yourself. You can build up a collection in your mind of certain techniques and preferences that you see other people do but you don't really start to learn until you're actually doing it yourself and you've done it for a little while on your own.*

Through participation and immersion into their respective working environments, industry professionals bring a rich mixture of recollection to exploring the apprenticeship process in the context of formal education. These reflections provide an opportunity to consider a wider skillset, that goes beyond developing musical and technical skills, to include social skills and openness to learning as considerations for inclusion in the toolbox.

ANALYSIS AND OUTCOMES.

The concept of the student - or indeed professional toolbox - provides an interesting metaphor for consideration of both the acquisition of these tools and the content of the toolbox. How well equipped such a toolbox is depends on a wide range of factors but the feeling of experienced professionals, graduate professionals and, to some extent, the students themselves, indicate that having the right tools to use at the right time is an essential part of being professional. In looking at the discussion of professional and student participants, it would seem that people, relationships and working as part of a team was an essential part of the toolbox. The toolbox metaphor also allows us to critically examine the effectiveness of the student toolkit in the context of the professional environment.

Situated learning is considered by Wenger as a way of immersing 'groups of people who share a concern, a set of problems or a passion about a topic, and who deepen their knowledge and expertise in this area by interacting on an on-going basis' (2002, 6). An element of this learning resides in the social nature of recording that comes from the daily interaction with people. As the entries in the notebook of a student on a one-year studio placement suggests, a key aspect was adapting to interacting with clients not only in the studio but outside where it was essential to promote the services of the studio to other potential clients.

From this viewpoint, the difference between situated learning and institutional learning could easily seen as a flaw in our provision. However, from a critical perspective, we might begin to take a wider perspective of the formal educational frameworks we use today and the agendas by which we measure our success. As we have tried to demonstrate, once embedded concepts such as the industry-ready agenda draw on deeply concepts which, as Ian Cross pointed out yesterday, have their roots in the 19th century with the apprenticeship model reaching much further back in our collective consciousness.

The link between the creative industries and the economy by successive governments since the 1990s has significantly narrowed the lens from which we not only view but *value* education. In setting his remit for the *Creative Industries Mapping Document* (1998) Chris Smith focused solely on the economic benefits. Had Smith read Bordieu's work he may have considered other forms of capital including cultural capital which may have 'promoted a wider appreciation of that value' (DCMS, 1998: 3). According to this report, 'total revenues of the music industry in 1995 were £3.6bn' and,

> *Sales of recorded music have been growing at a 10% annual compound growth rate...attributable to: the strength of domestic releases; the extension of music demand across three generations; increased buying power among older income groups; and favourable economic conditions in the UK. (1998, 68).*

While Smith was utilising already out of date sales figures as a means for justifying the importance of the creative economy, Pine and Gilmore

(1999) were formulating what they would call 'the experience economy', a model which argues that with technological progress, increasing competition and a shift in expectation of consumers shifts the focus from goods (tangible things) to an experience economy where products are given away as a way of not only selling services but providing experiences.

In a dynamic and changing industry, education provides some stability for students to develop the skills necessary for success. By looking to the past and considering those aspects of the apprenticeship model, which were essential for a career in the music industry, we might be in a better position to assess the success of our own courses. Our research indicates that for some students, the opportunity to work in an industry environment, simulated or not, provides an opportunity to place industry-essential tools in their metaphorical toolbox. Industry weeks, (real) client-led briefs and placements all contribute to the development of this metaphorical toolbox. However, our concerns go beyond the immediate tools and experiences. In reviewing the cultural industries in 1998, the DCMS used figures from 1995 and in doing so, completely ignored the potential of the Internet. In the same way, as educators, we have much to learn from the past but the context of that learning has to be focused on the future for it is at this point our students will engage with richer economies than the industry-education agenda suggests.

REFERENCES

Ashton, D. (2010). Productive passions and everyday pedagogies: Exploring the industry-ready agenda in higher education. In *Art, Design & Communication in Higher Education* 9 (1), 41–56.

Bakhshi, H., Hargreaves, I., & Mateos-Garcia, J. (2013). *A Manifesto for the Creative Economy*. London: Nesta. p. 103.

Boehm, C. (2006). The thing about the quotes: "Music Technology" degrees in Britain. In: *ICMC Conference Proceedings*, New Orleans, ICMA. *Retrieved from http://quod.lib.umich.edu/cgi/p/pod/dodidx?c=icmc;idno=bbp2372.2006.138*

Burnard, P. (2012). *Musical Creativities in Practice*. Oxford: OUP

Cohen, S. (1993). Ethnography and Popular Music Studies. *Popular Music* 12 (2), 123-138.

Creative and Cultural Skills. (2014). *Building a creative nation*. Retrieved from http://ccskills.org.uk/supporters/funding/details/the-creative-employment-programme

Department for Culture, Media and Sport. (1998). *Creative Industries Mapping Document.* London: DCMS Available at: http://www.culture.gov.uk/Reference_library/Publications/archive_1998/Creative_Industries_Mapping_Document_1998.htm

DTI and CEPR. (1999). The Economics of the Knowledge Driven Economy. *Conference Papers jointly organised by the Department of Trade and Industry and the Centre for Economic Policy Research London.* Retrieved from http://webarchive.nationalarchives.gov.uk/+/http://www.dti.gov.uk/comp/competitive/pdfs/kdeproc.pdf

Jewson, N. (2007). 'Communities of practice in their place: some implications of changes in the spatial location of work' in Jason Hughes, Nick Jewson and Lorna Unwin, eds. *Communities of Practice: Critical Perspectives* . London: Routledge. p. 156.

Lindlof, T. R. (1995). *Qualitative research methods.* Thousand Oaks: Sage.

Mitchell, S. (2014) How does the creative economy work? *Building a creative nation.* Retrieved from http://ccskills.org.uk/supporters/blog/how-does-the-creative-economy-work

National Advisory Committee on Creative and Cultural Education. (1999). *All Our Futures: Creativity, Culture and Education.* London: Department of Culture Media and Sport.

Pine, J. & Gilmore, J. (1999). *The Experience Economy,* Harvard Business School Press, Boston.

Thompson, P. & McIntyre, P. (2013). Rethinking creative practice in record production and studio recording education: addressing the field. In *Journal of the Art of Record Production.* Retrieved from http://arpjournal.com/2603/rethinking-creative-practice-in-record-production-and-studio-recording-education-addressing-the-field/

Unwin, L. (2007). English apprenticeship from past to present: The challenges and consequences of rampant 'community' diversity. In J. Hughes, N. Jewson and L. Unwin, (Eds.), *Communities of Practice: Critical Perspectives* . London: Routledge.

Wenger, E. McDrmott, R and Snyder, W. (2002). *Cultivating communities of practice: a guide to managing knowledge.* Boston: Harvard Business School Press. p. 6.

Williamson, J. & Cloonan, M. (2007). Rethinking the Music Industry. *Popular Music* 26/7. Cambridge: CUP. 305-322.

In a dynamic and changing industry, education provides some stability for students to develop the skills necessary for engagement with the industry at some level. The project uses the metaphor of a 'toolbox' as a way to examine the variety of skills and aptitudes essential for a career in the music industry by comparing past and present ways of preparing for a career in the recording industry. Our research indicates that for some students, the opportunity to work in an industry environment, simulated or not, provides an opportunity to place industry-essential tools in their metaphorical toolbox.

Our research indicates that for some students, the opportunity to work in an industry environment, simulated or not, provides an opportunity to place industry-essential tools in their metaphorical toolbox.

The Art of Practice: the crossroads between reflection, creativity and determination

‖ Monica Esslin-Peard

University of Liverpool, UK

‖ Tony Shorrocks

University of Liverpool, UK

ABSTRACT

In this paper, we explore the dichotomies between peer and teacher-directed learning in secondary and tertiary education. Much research has been conducted into the practice and performance habits of adult classical musicians, whilst some studies have looked at adult and professional performers from other musical genres. Our research goal was to investigate the practice and performance habits of secondary school students at a comprehensive school in a deprived urban town in the South East of England. Based on our research findings, we discuss effective models for teacher intervention – or non-intervention- to improve student progress and outcomes at KS4 and KS5 and consider the continuum between formal and informal learning for instrumentalists, singers and bands inside and outside the classroom. Current research at the University of Liverpool focuses on the relationship between reflective practice diaries, an annual reflective essay and the development of the aspiring professional musician in classical, popular and jazz music. Initial findings from the research suggest that keeping a practice diary and reflecting formally on progress increase levels of participation and retention over the three year undergraduate performance courses. Moreover, whilst classical and popular musicians exhibit different behaviours towards practice – in part due to the situated nature of learning in a band versus individual technical practice, chamber music or orchestral and big band playing and choral work, a pattern seems to be emerging that suggests that in the end, the majority of undergraduates develop an understanding of deliberate practice. Examples will be given of individual musicians – both classical and "other-than-classical" and we will consider the role of reflective learning in secondary and tertiary education, using practice diaries, individual performance assessments and reflective essays on practice and performance.

KEYWORDS

Performance, Practice, Reflection

AIMS AND METHODS

The goal of this research project is to discover using quantitative and qualitative analysis whether there is a direct relationship between the quality of reflection in practice diaries and the annual practice essay and the standard of performance in end-of-year recitals. Ethical approval has been gained to access student records, student reflective essays§ and performance grades for popular and classical musicians for the academic year 2013-2014, including access to their grades/essays from the academic year 2012-2013. A secondary area for investigation is the use of reflective journaling in the creative arts, and the degree of direction (or lack of direction) given to undergraduates with reference to their diaries and reflective essays. Whilst much has been written on reflective journaling in other academic areas, this research project allows us to explore the experiences of popular and classical musicians. A further consideration is the level of personal insight which each musician gains throughout the course. A possible model for their development is the Johari Window. An initial set of results from the data available will be presented at the conference.

IMPLICATIONS

The initial findings from this research project are relevant for university music departments in the UK and beyond as self-assessment is commonly required of undergraduates. We hope to give some pointers for effective reflection and the implications for the design of performance modules. This seminar is aimed at music academics and researchers, class music teachers, peripatetic music teachers, regional music hubs, university department staff and anyone interested in the musical development of young people. Monica Esslin-Peard is Director of Music at a secondary school in South East England and a doctoral research student at the University of Liverpool School of Music, specialising in Practice and Performance. Tony Shorrocks joined the University of Liverpool as Head of Performance after a long career as an orchestral player.

REFERENCES

Ghaye, T (2011) *Teaching and Learning through reflective practice.* Abingdon: Routledge

Lebler, D (2008) 'Popular music pedagogy: peer learning in practice'. *Music Education Research* 10 (2) 193-213.

Miksza, P (2011) 'A Review of Research on Practicing: Summary and Synthesis of the Extant Research with Implications for a new Theoretical Orientation.' *Bulletin of the Council for Research in Music Education.* 190 51-92.

Initial Teacher Education in England: Music Trainee Teachers' Development of Technology Skills

| Marina Gall

Graduate School of Education, University of Bristol, UK

| Nick Breeze

University of Worcester, UK

Abstract

This paper presents the intermediate findings of a current research project that aims to consider in depth the development of current student music teachers' music technology-related skills. Located in the southwest of England, the study is founded upon the authors' previous teaching and research. Having recently worked together closely, supporting trainee music teachers on a one year secondary Postgraduate Certificate in Education (PGCE) course, both have completed Ph.Ds that focus on children's use of music technology. Their research has explored Information and Communications Technology (ICT) and music in schools, including the work of practising teachers (Gall & Breeze, 2007; Gall, Lazarus, Tidmarsh & Breeze, 2009) and music technology in teacher education across Europe (Gall, Rotar Pance, Brändström, Stöger & Sammer, 2011; Gall, Sammer & de Vugt, 2012; Sammer, Gall & Breeze, 2009). Most recently, Gall's research has focussed upon initial teacher trainees' perceptions of what hindered them in their ICT work whilst on school placements (Gall, 2013). This experience is focused here upon a representative sample of students currently undertaking a one-year post-graduate course for secondary music teachers and through undertaking six case studies, seeks to investigate how the students' technological and pedagogical skills can be best developed and how their experiences compare with those of other students across Europe.

KEYWORDS

Music technology, trainee teachers, pedagogic skills

AIMS

This study aims to address two research questions "How can new music teachers' technological and pedagogic skills be best developed to promote music learning?" and "How do these trainee music teachers' experiences compare and contrast with those across Europe".

METHODS

The research, undertaken from a social constructivist perspective (Vygotsky, 1978), focuses on six case studies of student teachers completing a one-year secondary classroom music teacher course[*] at one higher education institution. Three teaching placements are undertaken during the course, the second of which is in progress at the time of writing. The participants consisted of three males and three females; two participants were skilled in the use of technology at the start of the course, two arrived on the course with some skills and two classified themselves as complete beginners. Following the completion of an initial ICT questionnaire, which sought to ascertain participants' perceptions of their own abilities, the case study students have been completing reflective journals throughout the course, noting: 1. the development of their ICT and pedagogic skills: a. in their own time; b. within university session; c. during school placements. 2. their feelings and attitudes towards music technology and ICT within school music. [etwpara]Further data is also drawn from students' formal course evaluations, observations of their teaching, including school mentor feedback and discussion, and formal assessment documents. [*]In England, students intending to teach at secondary level typically study their subject for 3 years and then complete a one-year teacher education course.

OUTCOMES

An intermediate analysis of the questionnaire and the reflective journals has revealed some emerging issues. The questionnaire showed that although most students had used music ICT at school, only one had used it as part of their degree course and none had observed any outstanding work with music ICT in the classroom prior to starting the course. Some more general points that arose included the relationship of music ICT to the music curriculum and the purposes of its use, particularly accessibility. The trainee teacher journals confirmed that the University technology sessions at all levels (ranging from those with no experience of music technology to advanced users) were valued by all students, although less experienced students have reported elsewhere that they would have valued greater ICT time and support. Upon starting their first school placements, students' confidence appeared to vary in line with their perceived abilities. All except one were involved with teaching using music ICT, with one comment made by a less experienced student about their level of competence being only just adequate; however there were several comments about music ICT not being available to Key Stage 3 students (ages 11-14) at some schools, owing principally to a lack of resources. Students' confidence about their second school placements mirrored their attitudes at the time of their first placement. As before, most students were able to use music ICT in their classes, including part of one formal assignment, in which a series of lessons is based on the use of music ICT. It was clear from the diaries that less experienced students were able to teach successful lessons that used music ICT and it could be seen in their assignment evaluations that they were engaging with the appropriate issues related to the pedagogy of teaching using music ICT, such as the design of worksheets (in order to provide all the necessary information clearly), the use of teacher time, the usefulness of pupils sharing their work, the design of the sequencer template, the prior checking of resources to ensure the compatibility of sequencer file versions, the importance of headphones and the correct identification of the time required by pupils to complete tasks. Other interesting issues to emerge not immediately related to the research questions included the use of iPads for classroom music learning (which would appear to be increasing) and the resourcing necessary for all pupils to engage with music ICT.

EPILOGUE

At the conclusion of this project, we expect to provide full results and analysis, that we hope will not only further the use of music ICT in the classroom, but will help future teacher educators to prepare the next generation of teachers for the challenges that lie ahead. This current paper focuses upon our first research question; we also intend to use our findings from the English context as a basis for further comparative study with practices across other European countries.

REFERENCES

Gall, M., Rotar Pance, B., Brändström, S., Stöger, C. & Sammer, G. (2011). Learning from each other: Music Teacher Training in Europe. In G-B. von Carlsburg, A. Liimets & A.

Gaizutis (Eds.) *Music Inside and Outside The School*. Baltische Studien zur Erziehungs - und Sozialwissenschaft, Frankfurt: Peter Lang GmbH, pp.325-344.

Gall, M., Sammer, G. & de Vugt, A. (Eds.) (2012). *European Perspectives on Music Education: New Media in the Classroom*. Innsbruck: Helbling Verlagsgesellschaft mbH.

Gall, M. (2013). Trainee Teachers' Perceptions: Factors that Constrain the Use of Music Technology in Teaching Placements. *Journal of Music, Technology and Education.* 6(1), pp.5-27.

Gall, M. & Breeze, N. (2007). The subculture of music and ICT in the classroom. *Technology, Pedagogy & Education.* 16(1), pp.41-56.

Gall, M., Lazarus, E., Tidmarsh, C. & Breeze, N. (2009). Creative designs for learning. In R. Sutherland, P. John & S. Robertson (Eds.) *Improving Classroom Learning with ICT*. London: Routledge, pp.88-114.

Sammer, G., Gall, M. & Breeze, N. (2009) Using Music software in school: The European framework. In G. Fiocchetta & F. Ballanti (Eds.) *NET MUSIC Project 01: New Technology in the Field of Education (Nuove Tecnologie in Campo Educativo Musicale)*. Rome: Anicia srl, pp.155-177. Available online at: http://tinyurl.com/npeb9gq (Accessed 13 January 2014)

Vygotsky, L. (1978) *Mind in Society*. London: Harvard University Press.

Collaborative music production in a virtual learning environment: An experience with English and Spanish students

Andrea Giraldez Hayes
Universidad de Valladolid, Spain

David Carabias Galindo
Universidad de Valladolid, Spain

ABSTRACT

The development of online collaborative tools, made feasible by the expansion of computer network systems and communication technologies, has opened new possibilities for music composition. The authors describe a series of small collaborative music production projects developed between a group of Secondary School students in London (UK) and a group of undergraduate music teachers in Segovia (Spain) using virtual learning environment: OpenSounds.

KEYWORDS

Collaborative music composition, Virtual learning environment, Transnational interaction

AIMS

To explore the possibilities of an online learning environment for music composition. To analyse the musical and verbal interaction between groups of students of different ages and cultural backgrounds.

METHODS

Two groups of MYP3 and MYP4 students from London (UK) and a group of undergraduate music teachers from Segovia (Spain) participated in this exploratory qualitative study. Although participant observation was used to understand the individual behaviour during the lessons, the most important data (music compositions and verbal interaction) was collected on the virtual learning platform (OpenSounds) and used to analyse the development of social connections, the learners' participation and the impact of collaborative music composing and social interaction on students' engagement. Some semi-structured interviews were also conducted with the teachers and some students registered in Opensounds.

OUTCOMES

Four themes emerged from the data analysis with reference to the research questions. The findings in the study indicate that (a) the use of an online learning environment can be an important factor of motivation among students, (b) a good relationship and respect comes from participating in collaborative productions, (c) social interaction can facilitate online learning in a variety of ways, (d) some students can improve their music composition and skills through the interaction with pairs. Some limitations from the experienced were also acknowledged in order to improve future projects.

IMPLICATIONS

This exploratory study provides some insights to plan different actions for teachers and lecturers using this kind of virtual learning environments with their students and offers an outlook of the possibilities of transnational music composition in collaborative projects developed among students of different ages and backgrounds.

ACKNOWLEDGEMENTS

International Community School (London, UK) for giving us the possibility to do this research with their students.

REFERENCES

Seddon, F. (2009). Music e-learning environments: Young people, composing and the Internet. In J. Finney & P. Burnard (Eds.). *Music Education with Digital Technology*. London: Continuum International Group.

Himonides, E. (2012). The Misundertanding of Music-Technology-Education: A Meta Perspective. In G. McPherson & G. Welch (Eds.), *The Oxford Handbook of Music Education [Vol. 2]* (pp. 433-456). Oxford: Oxford University Press.

Salavuo, M. (2006). Open and informal online communities as forums of collaborative musical activities and learning, *British Journal of Music Education*, 23, 253–271.

An Exploratory Study of the Effect of an Eye Guide While Sight Playing at the Piano

▌ Sara Hagen
    Valley City State University, USA

▌ Walter Boot
    Florida State University, USA

▌ Vicki McArthur
    Florida State University, USA

▌ Cynthia Stephens-Himonides
    University of London Institute of Education, UK

▌ Alejandro Cremaschi
    University of Colorado--Boulder, USA

ABSTRACT

Sight-reading at the piano is a skill that virtually all collegiate class piano instructors deem essential in the development of music majors with performance specialties other than piano. Most students in this situation find sight playing difficult and finding ways to improve their performance is not an easy matter as sight-reading performance itself is a set of many skills. Several models have been proposed to understand the process of sight-reading (Kopiez, Weihs, Ligges, & Lee, 2006; Thompson and Lehmann, 2004; Utdaisuk, 2005) in which perceptual, cognitive, and psychomotor processes along with musical expertise and experience have been examined as predictors of sight-reading performance. Differences in eye movements (saccades) and when the eyes are relatively still (fixations) have been found between expert and novice sight-readers. Early studies found that better readers required shorter and fewer fixations, during which time information is perceived and processed, and more notes per fixation (Jacobsen, 1942; Weaver, 1943). Goolsby (1994a, 1994b) found that skilled readers fixated on blank areas of the score rather than each note. He also found that less skilled readers more likely fixated on notes and rests. Skilled pianists were found to have a larger span (two beats) than less skilled pianists (half a beat) (Furneaux & Land, 1999; Gillman & Underwood, 2003). Surprisingly, skilled and less skilled sight-readers do not significantly differ in perceptual span, which is the amount of written notation extracted around the fixation point (Raynor & Pollatsek, 1997; Truitt, Clifton, Pollastsek, & Raynor, 1997; Gilman and Underwood, 2003). Yet, the fixations of good sight-readers jump around the score and expand across line and phrase boundaries, not just individual notes, suggesting that they are not just looking ahead, but ahead and back. The distance between the eyes and hands of skilled sight-readers (eye-hand span) is larger than less skilled readers (Gillman & Underwood, 2003; Goolsby, 1994a; Rayner & Pollastsek, 1997; Truitt, et al, 1997). "Generally speaking, a phenomenon of reading ahead is a behavioral consequence of a well-developed psychological readiness of the larger eye-hand span" (Udtaisuk, p. 119). The "multi-tasking" skill of sight-reading includes playing current measure, scanning the next measure, using analytical ability for memory and recall, comprehending the music, and moving fingers to find the keys without looking at the keyboard, all of which fits with the models described earlier. Eye movement is not only the result of trained eyes, but also of perceptual ability, or the ability to group notes into a meaningful pattern (Lehmann & McArthur, 2002). More experienced sight-readers remember longer sequences and can perceive multiple details of the musical score as a single piece of information than less skilled players (Goolsby, 1994; Thompson & Lehmann, 2004). As reported by Hagen (2001), the computer has been used mostly as a collection device in sight-reading research rather than as a teaching aid, yet when used for teaching, computer-assisted instruction has been shown to be equal to traditional methods and possibly advantageous. The use of technology to develop group piano student keyboard skills has been investigated (Benson, 2002, Sheldon, Reese, & Grashel, 1998; Tomzcak, 1999,Watkins, 1984). There have been some investigations of the use of technology to improve sight-reading skills in group piano classes. The use of MIDI accompaniment disks to develop harmonization and sight-reading skills was not found to have an effect on either of these skills, but was helpful for motivational practice (Betts and Cassidy, 2000). Hagen (2001) compared the effectiveness of three practice methods, of which two were computer-assisted, on sight-reading at the piano. One program used a play-along accompaniment practice method (Finale), while the other was for chord recognition practice (Harmony). A third group used traditional classroom instruction. Comparing the rhythm and note accuracy among the three groups, the only significant difference found was for note accuracy with the Finale group performing better. As the review of literature revealed, good sight-readers' eye movements have shorter and fewer fixations and move forward and backward which is a result of perceptual ability. Less skilled sight-readers correct mistakes and have a shorter eye-hand span. Could novice sight-readers' skills be developed partly through focusing their attention (eyes) on forward movement in the score? With the development of play-along computer software programs, eye guides, whether or not for the purpose of developing sight-reading skills, can be found and are commercially available. No studies were found that compared the use of computer software programs, which utilize an eye guide during playback or play-along accompaniment of a piece. There are many studies of eye movement while performing music reading activities, however, there are no explorations of the effect of an eye guide while reading from a digital score while sight playing at the piano. The question posed in this pilot study of 15 participants: "What effect would a sweeping eye guide have on eye movements in beginning university class piano students?" Participants read 8-measure grand staff melodies with left hand accompaniment patterns with and without a sweeping eye guide produced in software such as Finale. This initial question was answered with two significant results between having an eye guide present or not. Music reading with the eye guide for a subgroup of eight participants whose data was complete indicated significantly longer fixations ($F(1,7) = 9.78$, $p < .05$, partial eta squared = .58) and significantly fewer eye movements ($F(1,7) = 8.21$, $p < .05$, partial eta squared = .54). A discussion of the process, the significant differences, an interpretation of these differences, and suggestions for future research in this area will be presented.

KEYWORDS

eye guide, sight playing, eye movements

AIMS

The purpose of this study was to explore the efficacy of studying the effects of eye guides on allocation of attendance as evidenced by eye movements while music reading at the computer while performing a sight playing activity. The researchers realize the coarseness of this pursuit, but felt that this initial activity might provide reasonable data to move ahead on a larger, more carefully crafted and financed study. Many recent studies were used as the basis of the trial, including the research team's own collaborative studies previously conducted in the area of sight playing at the piano. The initial question was simply to determine if there was any effect on eye movement with a guide present. The hypothesis: the eye guide will affect the allocation of attendance of pianists during a sightplaying task. Since tracking eye movement while reading music with an eye guide has never been tested, the degree to which the eyes are guided or distracted is unknown. Past research without the use of an eye tracker by the same researchers has found no significant difference among groups with eye guides present toward improvement of performance over time; however, a preference for the sweeping vertical eye guide was found. The next logical step in determining the effectiveness of an eye guide is to observe how the eye is moving in relation to the guide. Further investigation may provide insights into how the guides might be used as tools for training the eye to continually move forward, a typical issue with beginning sight-readers.

METHODS

Subjects (N=15) were selected from the lowest sight-reading skill bracket from a first-year university piano class in order to test the novice eyes, which were hypothesized to be the most distractible. Before the experiment, participants placed their chin on a chin rest and an Eyelink 1000 Eyetracker (SR Research, http://www.eyelinkinfo.com/index.php) was calibrated to record eye movements during the experiment. This desk-mounted eye tracking system uses a video camera to determine which objects participants are looking at. The calibration process took between 2 and 5 minutes. During this period of time, participants were asked to look at a series of dots that appeared at nine different locations on the computer monitor. After an initial calibration period in which eye position was calibrated to screen coordinates, each participant's right eye was sampled at a rate of 1000 Hz by an EyeLink 1000 eyetracking system (SR Research, Inc.). An eye movement was classified as a saccade if its amplitude exceeded .2° and either a) its velocity exceeded 30 degs/sec or b) its acceleration exceeded 9500 degs/sec_. A chin and forehead rest minimized head movements and maintained a constant viewing distance (approximately 73 cm). Two sources of data were obtained: and eye data file with the X and Y position of each participant's gaze and video of what the participant viewed with his or her gaze superimposed on top, along with a timestamp corresponding to the events in the eye data file. This allowed for the extraction of precise eye movement parameters for each relevant playing period from the eye data file. Video and audio recordings of the performance were also obtained. In addition, participants were able to orient themselves to the piano, playing a five-finger scale and chord pattern in the key in which they will be playing. Subjects played two short piano pieces with and without the sweeping vertical eye guide present while hearing a metronomic "tick." Subjects were told in advance in which order they will perform the task and had an opportunity to rest in between performances if desired. The participants signed an agreement to participate voluntarily and were paid $8 for their time. All participants sightread two musical selections within the playing ability of the class, each with and without an eye guide present. This pattern was repeated in a different order to counterbalance order effect. All pieces were played at the same tempo, set with a countoff of one measure at the beginning and a metronome throughout. A subgroup (n=8) was selected sets of data were selected based on the completeness of the data collected. Tests were run to determine the number of fixations, length of fixations, and number of regressive saccades.

Outcomes

Several of the participants experienced some sort of anomaly in the procedures, excluding them from the study, such as interference of eyewear or computer malfunction. Therefore a subset of eight participants was used for statistical analysis. Recognizing that this group is small, nonetheless significant differences were found in the number and length of fixations between the guide and no-guide examples. The music reading activities with eye guides showed fewer eye movements ($F(1,7) = 8.21$, $p < .05$, partial eta squared $= .54$) and longer fixation durations ($F(1,7) = 9.78$, $p < .05$, partial eta squared $= .58$). Further exploration comparing performances and reviewing placements of fixations on the score may provide further insights into the findings. In addition, an order effect will be studied in more detail to see what effect the performance of each piece 4 different times has on eye movements. Eye movement evidence suggests that an eye guide does indeed influence the allocation of attention as evidenced by changes in scanning with and without the guide. The pattern of longer fixations but fewer eye movements suggests a more efficient scanning pattern in which players extract more information during each fixation. Additional analyses and research will be necessary to confirm this explanation. Longitudinal studies of the acquisition of sight reading skill can help determine whether these changes in scanning are functional and whether they facilitate the development of sight reading ability over time.

Discussion

Further exploration comparing performances and reviewing placements of fixations on the score may provide further insights into the findings. In addition, an order effect will be studied in more detail to see what effect the performance of each piece 4 different times has on eye movements. Eye movement evidence suggests that an eye guide does indeed influence the allocation of attention as evidenced by changes in scanning with and without the guide. The pattern of longer fixations but fewer eye movements suggests a more efficient scanning pattern in which players extract more information during each fixation. Additional analyses and research will be necessary to confirm this explanation. Longitudinal studies of the acquisition of sight reading skill can help determine whether these changes in scanning are functional and whether they facilitate the development of sight reading ability over time.

Acknowledgements

A special thank you to The Florida State University for its support through faculty and research assistant time, facilities, and equipment.

References

Kopiez, R., Weihs, C., Ligges, U., & Lee, J (2006). Classification of high and low achievers in a music sight-reading task. *Psychology of Music*, 34(1), 5-26.

Thompson, S. and Lehmann, A. (2004). Strategies for sight-reading and improvising music. In Aaron Williamon (Ed.), *Musical Excellence: Strategies and techniques to enhance performance* (pp. 143-159). Oxford: University Press.

Goolsby, T. W. (1994). Eye movement in music reading: Effects of reading ability, notational complexity, and encounters. *Music Perception*, 12, 77-96.

Technology-mediated feedback in advanced level piano learning of ABEGG Variations by Schumann: an exploratory pilot study

‖ Luciana Hamond

Institute of Education, University of London, UK

Abstract

There is evidence that the application of modern technology can be beneficial in instrumental and vocal learning in Higher Education. However, what is not yet clear is how technology can be used in and be integrated into a piano lesson in order to enhance student's learning. Consequently, an exploratory pilot study was undertaken in the UK in order to investigate more systematically the pedagogical use of technology in a piano studio. The participants were an advanced piano student, an expert piano teacher, and a researcher (the author). Technology-mediated feedback was used to foster the improvement of the ABEGG Variations by Schumann in two piano lessons. Data collection involved the video recorded observation of the piano lessons, followed by audio recorded interviews with participants (teacher and student) separately after the lessons. The technology involved in the lesson was a digital piano, connected to a laptop computer with software (Cockos' Reaper) using a MIDI interface. Real-time and post-hoc feedback regarding particular aspects of the performance, such as articulation, dynamics, timing, and pedalling, was provided to the participants using an additional computer screen. Data analysis involved the use of the software for qualitative data analysis NVivo10 for observed data and interview data. The observed data was analysed in three dimensions (behaviours including feedback, focus content, and piano pedagogical approaches) and compared to the interview data and to the researcher's perception.

Keywords

feedback, technology, piano pedagogy

AIMS

The intention of this exploratory pilot study is to investigate more systematically the pedagogical use of technology in a piano studio, in this case to enhance the performance of ABEGG Variations by Schumann.

METHODS

An exploratory pilot study was undertaken. Participants were a piano teacher (Brazilian, female), a piano student (Brazilian, male), and a researcher (Brazilian, female). Two piano lessons with technology-mediated feedback was conducted followed by interviews. In the lessons, teacher and student were asked about specific refinements and possible improvements that they were seeking in the ABEGG Variations whilst the researcher was operating the assistive technology. Each teaching session was 1h18min long, and was followed by interviews with teacher (29 min and 21 min), and with student (26 min and 15 min), respectively for each session. Technology-mediated feedback was used in real-time, and in post-hoc. Two approaches were used for the data collection: video observation of two piano lessons and audio recorded interviews. Qualitative data analysis involved the use of the software NVivo10 and encompassed: (1) transcribing video and audio recordings; (2) coding themes for three dimensions (behaviours including feedback, focus content, and piano pedagogy approach); and (3) comparing observed data and interview data.

OUTCOMES

The observed data was analysed in three dimensions. The first dimension showed all behaviours (including feedback) common to one-to-one piano setting, such as student's and teacher's verbal and non-verbal behaviours. However, the observed data also included other behaviours unique to these sessions such as: (a) researcher verbal and non-verbal behaviours; (b) technology-mediated feedback; (c) listening and seeing the computer screen; and (d) and pointing to the computer screen. The second dimension demonstrated the focus content for these particular sessions such as: (a) Identifying learning needs; (b) Making relations between image and sound; (c) Making suggestions or giving ideas on the use of technology; (d) Being Aware of what is happening (in the performance); (e) Negotiating direction or focus; (f) Negative perspectives (e.g. digital piano); (g) Positive perspectives (e.g. performance analysis); (h) Reporting previous experiences; and (i) Commenting on student's emotional state. The third dimension involved the piano pedagogical approach foci whilst using the technology: (1) articulation (legato); (2)

timing (evenness, note duration and note asynchrony); (3) technique (imbalance within one hand and between hands, shortening a chord or an octave before a leap, and lapsing thumb); (4) pedaling (changing, mixing or late pedaling); (5) dynamics (voicing the octaves); and (6) melody and note accuracy (wrong notes, missing notes, or lapsing thumb note). From the interview data it was revealed that the use of this technology in these two teaching sessions appears to show the information about the performance in a much clearer way, it can alert on musical and technical aspects not commonly revealed in a traditional piano studio environment, and it can also support teacher feedback, according to the student. Likewise, the teacher reported that this technology-mediated feedback appears to promote greater attention by associating image and sound, it can support identifying student's learning needs, and it can help a better understanding of what and why a learning difficulty is happening. As participant-observer researcher, my perspective is that using this technology can approximate teacher's and student's views on student's learning needs, and it can also promote an agreement between them. In addition, technology-mediated feedback in an advanced level piano studio might have an impact not only on student's learning process but also on the teacher's pedagogical approach.

IMPLICATIONS

The findings of this exploratory pilot study might not be generalized because it is context-specific. It also depends on the repertoire, and on the individual differences of participants. For this particular exploratory pilot study, the use of this technology in these two sessions seemed to make both, but more importantly the student, more conscious on the student's learning needs. In conclusion, it seems that technology-mediated feedback appears not only to support teacher pedagogical approach as an additional tool for an effective teaching but it also appears to improve student's self-awareness on own performance by identifying learning needs. Limitations of this exploratory pilot study included the use of digital piano for advanced level piano performances, the difficult visualization for complex variations, technical software problems, and limited knowledge on technology by the researcher. The effective pedagogical use of technology for advanced level piano learning continues to be explored in current fieldwork.

ACKNOWLEDGEMENTS

Professor Graham F. Welch and Dr. Evangelos Himonides for their support during my PhD journey. The Brazilian Foundation CAPES (Higher Education Coordination Agency) for supporting my PhD study.

REFERENCES

Burwell, K. (2010). *Instrumental teaching and learning in Higher Education*. Unpublished PhD thesis. University of Kent.

Howard, D. M., Brereton, J., Welch, G. F., Himonides, E., Decosta, M., Williams, J., and Howard, A. W. (2007). "Are real-time displays of benefit in the singing studio? An exploratory study." *Journal of Voice*, 21(1), 20-34.

Welch, G. F., Howard, D. M., Himonides, E., and Brereton, J. (2005). "Real-time feedback in the singing studio: an innovatory action-research project using new voice technology." *Music Education Research*, 7(2), 225-249.

Musical gameplay: a theoretical exploration

❙❙ Sigrid Jordal Havre
    Sibelius Academy, University of the Arts, Finland
    Bergen University College, Norway

❙ Lauri Väkevä
    Sibelius Academy, University of the Arts, Finland

Abstract

The word "play" has different meanings in research literature, referring to a variety of activities with different functions and purposes. In this paper, we take a look at how different concepts of play could help us to understand entertainment music gaming as learning activity. Instead of looking at music itself as a playful activity in education, we consider it from the standpoint of play and game theory, using musical entertainment games as references. Our aim is to construct a theoretical background for understanding how playing entertainment games can communicate musical meaning, form musical attitudes, and evoke musical actions through signs, rules and performance.

Keywords

Music education, Play, Game

Aims

This paper takes a look at how different concepts of play can help to understand entertainment music gaming as learning activity. Our aim is to construct a theoretical background for comprehending how entertainment games can communicate musical meaning, form musical attitudes, and evoke musical actions.

METHODS

This article is a literature-based theoretical exploration.

OUTCOMES

Psychological research has a long tradition of describing play as form of cognitive processing. Vygotsky (1933/1978) considered play as a key activity for child development. He described different stages of play, such as role-play, imaginary play, and competitive play, arguing for their different functions in cognitive development. Mead (1934/2009) argued that the child develops an understanding of society through role-play. Imitating the others, and reacting to her own actions, the child develops a sense of herself. In turn, game-playing organizes the attitudes of the players into a coordinated unit. Gaming can thus be seen as indicative of an ability to internalize social norms as basis of communal actions. Such ability is needed for developing a self capable of joining the others in "organized, co-operative social activity". From Huizinga's (1955) cultural-historical standpoint, play can be seen as unforced action that opens up a "temporary world within the ordinary world, dedicated to the performance of an act apart". Play produces a "magic circle" that absorbs the player, rewarding her intrinsic motivation without any "material interest". Play also promotes social groupings that "tend to surround themselves with secrecy and ... stress the difference from the common world". Sutton-Smith (1997) defines play as an activity that incorporates free choice and offers "escape". Playing can amount to social bonding, but it can also be sheer fun. However, every play is individual and needs to be considered in relation to the player's experience as well as to the social-cultural context. Caillois (1958) presents two play-styles; paidia, or spontaneous free-form play, and ludus, or formal play. A fundamental principle of play is that it is voluntary, immediate source of joy and amusement: forced play would cease to be play, for it would lose its playful characteristics. In game research literature, play is often described as the major element of the game (Caillois 1958; Juul 2005; Salen and Zimmermann 2004). Salen and Zimmerman (2004) make a distinction between "arbitrary" and "meaningful" play. Meaningful play indicates "the process by which a player takes action within the designed system ... [that] responds to the action". According to Juul (2005), games blend rules with imaginative play. The fictional world of play can be seen as a set of signs that cue the players into imagining different game scenarios (Juul 2005). Frasca (2007) defines play as an "activity in which the player believes to have active participation and interprets it as constraining her immediate future to a set of probable scenarios". In turn, game is a "form of play where players agree on a system of rules that assigns social status to their ... performance". Frasca thus frames game as both an object and an activity. With this focus, he attempts to answer not only to the question of "what are games?" but also "how are games?" One way of looking at "how games are" is to see them as learning activities. Both games and their cultural contexts can be seen as affinity spaces where relations between gamers are based on mutual interests. Affinity spaces are characterized by the intertwined concepts of play, performance, experimentation, interpretation, teaching, and learning (Gee 2004; Jenkins 2009). Hence, they can be seen as pedagogical environments that cater for personal growth through participation in meaningful activities in the gaming communities. Mäyrä (2008) suggests meaning of gaming is based on the combination of semiosis, or representation, and ludosis, or playful action. Play is important for games: it is important that one has freedom to choose one's strategies within the bounds of the game's rules. Freedom in gaming is also embedded in the affinity spaces: these spaces allow the gamers relative freedom to experiment with different strategies in relation to the actions of the other gamers. Importantly, gaming also provides room for mistakes: thus, gaming can be seen as an explorative activity that seeks new opportunities of making sense of conjoint actions. Musical learning can take place in many ways in entertainment gaming. One such way is constructing music-related knowledge e.g., by solving musical puzzles or learning to use digital tools to perform and create new music. Gameplay can also be oriented towards developing specific musical skills, such as singing, instrument playing or dancing (Collins 2008, 2012; Miller 2012). Some music games can even convey meanings that can lead to a change in the player_s views on music: such games encourage people to play with their own expectations by experimenting with new creative technologies and techniques. Musical gameplay encourages self-expression by enabling players to interact with existing music, to manipulate and experiment with musical elements, and to construct new musical creations. Gameplay can also develop abilities to recycle existing musical patterns for new purposes. Music games provide visual and auditive signs and symbols conveying meanings that assists and guide the players' intertwined actions. The rules of the game frame what is possible to explore and create in the game; in turn, metarules regulate how players can modify the rules. Even though game's rules regulate play on many levels, in the end it is the players' interpretation of the rules that individualize the gaming experience.

IMPLICATIONS

Understanding entertainment music games as educational learning environments can open one way to understand the relationship between play and meaning in musical learning. Exploring the play aspect of music gaming may also lead to a general understanding of the educative and expressive possibilities of the gaming media. Playing music and playing games intersect, as both have the capacity for immersive engagement, for structuring the musical experience, and for employing imagination.

REFERENCES

Huizinga, J. (1955). *Homo Ludens: A study of the play-element in culture.* Boston: Beacon Press.

Mead, G. H. (1934). *Mind, self & society, edited and introduced by C. Morris.* Chicago: University of Chicago Press.

Salen, K. and Zimmermann, E. (2004). *Rules of play: Game design fundamentals.* Cambridge, Massachusetts: The MIT Press.

A constructivist model for opening minds to sound-based music

|| David Holland

De Montfort University, U.K.

ABSTRACT

Students often find sound-based music (an umbrella term created by Leigh Landy to describe music where sound is the basic unit, rather than the musical note (Landy, 2007, p. 17)) difficult to understand when they first encounter it and this paper explores a practice-based method for increasing engagement through learning heightened listening skills. Accepting sound rather than notes as the basic unit of music can unlock access to a whole range of works and creative possibilities, but often this seems problematic for students. It therefore represents a 'threshold concept' in terms of the creative practice and appreciation of sound-based music. Traditional models of music education tend to focus on playing 'significant works' to students when introducing new musical concepts. This paper argues that a praxial approach (as advocated by Thomas Regelski (2002)) that allows the students to learn through creative practice can be much more effective in helping them to understand and appreciate sound-based music. The approach outlined in this paper utilizes a constructivist view of education where learners construct their own knowledge through their own activities. It is suggested that overcoming ingrained preconceptions of what 'music' should be (what could be regarded as 'troublesome knowledge' in relation to threshold concepts) might be better achieved through a model that allows students to discover the potential of sound-based music through their own compositional work rather than through traditional methods of learning.

KEYWORDS

Sound, Listening, Constructivism

Aims

This paper aims to offer a method for opening minds to sound-based music that involves participation in the creative process. Sound-based music usually involves material that is recorded or electronically created, which can then be manipulated and arranged for listening through loudspeakers. However, as this music is practiced mostly within the confines of academia, it can often seem strange and unfamiliar when encountered for the first time with listeners finding it difficult to understand. Sound-based music could therefore represent what Meyer and Land call a threshold concept (Meyer and Land, 2003). Central to the notion of threshold concepts is that it represents a 'transformed understanding' that opens up a new way of thinking about something (Meyer and Land, 2003, p. 1). Understanding sound-based music can require a change in ingrained expectations of what music can be, as sound-based music can seem alien to children's current conception of music and so represents what Meyer and Land describe as 'troublesome knowledge' (Meyer and Land, 2003:9). This paper aims to examine the challenge of opening children's minds to sound-based music through the theory of threshold concepts utilising a constructivist approach. Constructivism has become increasingly influential in education and argues for learning where the student constructs their own knowledge through group and individual activities. Additionally, those unfamiliar with this music often need guidance with how best to listen to it, so the paper aims to explain how listening training could aid creative practice in sound-based music.

Methods

As a means for enabling creative practice in sound-based music this paper proposes using 'heightened listening' as a compositional tool. This builds on my MA research (Holland, 2011), which indicated that heightened listening could be used in schools as an access tool for electroacoustic music. In this research, heightened listening was defined as a close concentration on the qualities of sounds that also allows for external associations to be made by the listener in relation to the sounds source. The research also suggested that allowing more participation in the creative process would have further increased engagement with the music for the children involved. This supports the constructivist argument by proposing that students might more easily engage with this music by experiencing first hand how sounds might be arranged musically using audio editing software, thereby constructing their own understanding of the music and its possibilities. This paper proposes a practice-based series of workshops where Key Stage 2 children can learn to use heightened listening as a tool to help them record sounds, which they can then use in their own sound-based compositions. In doing so it suggests a method that could be developed as a way to help pupils understand sound-based music as a threshold concept.

OUTCOMES

The apparent shift in emphasis to constructivism using practice-based learning in much recent research on music education and technology (for example, Higgins and Jennings, 2006; Savage and Challis, 2002) suggests that this could be a suitable method for opening learners minds to the creative possibilities of sound-based music. As Regelski (2002) acknowledges, traditional methods of music education seem out of touch offering up 'museum pieces' for students to passively listen to, whereas the inclusion of sound pieces in the curriculum can open up their ears to possibilities well beyond the aesthetic principles of western classical music (Regelski, 2002, p. 40).

IMPLICATIONS

Learning to compose sound pieces can develop students' skills in communicating through sound in general. Therefore, these skills will be useful for all types of music as well as helping to develop practice in new areas of music. Also, this type of music can provide a unique opportunity to allow pupils with little previous musical experience to creatively explore communication through sound and therefore build musical confidence in students of all abilities. It gives students the opportunity to discover the potential of sound-based music for themselves from 'within' the music itself. It is then that the concepts and theories that shape the aesthetic decisions made by composers of previous sound-based works become relevant and students, with guidance, can discover them in relation to their own work. Research suggests (such as Higgins and Jennings, 2006; Holland, 2011) that students can respond positively to sound-based music, and that this could be enhanced through a practice-based method that uses heightened listening as a means for new composers to build a relationship with their sound materials. Such an approach could enable students to overcome the threshold concept of using sounds, rather than musical notes, as their primary musical material.

REFERENCES

Landy, L. (2007). *Understanding the Art of Sound Organization.* Cambridge: Massachusetts Institute of Technology

Meyer, J.H.F. and Land, R. (2003). Threshold concepts and troublesome knowledge: linkages to ways of thinking and practicing. In *Enhancing Teaching-Learning Environments in Undergraduate Courses Project, Occasional Report 4*. Retrieved from http://www.etl.tla.ed.ac.uk//docs/ETLreport4.pdf

Regelski, T.A. (2002). Sound compositions for expanding musicianship education. *Organised Sound*, 7 (1), 29-40.

Audio Researchers: Are We Not Listening?

▌ Andrew Horsburgh

    Southampton Solent University, United Kingdom

ABSTRACT

Technology has created, adapted, and dictated significant changes throughout the history of music recording [1]. Recent research has furthered our understanding of the auditory mechanics and psychoacoustics [2], methods of qualitative assessment in music [2], and whilst tracking the progression of music's relationship with technology [1]. This paper hopes to raise a debate that the audio market is not listening to research, or if audio researchers have stopped listening to consumers? The paper provides a basis for this debate through results collected in a qualitative assessment of surround sound formats. Early results indicate responder numbers listening to surround sound are significantly reduced from the experimenters expectations. Spatial audio formats exploit the intersection of creative recording engineers and technology by develop a sense of immersion, realism, and excitement. Researchers working with in ideal conditions with simulations of sources in controlled input situations have demonstrated the superiority of surround formats when compared directly to existing stereophonic technology. More recently, a research project supported the theoretical research with data verifying that despite the superiority of technology. The central audio format was ambisonics. The format was developed to provide spatial freedoms and creativity by Gerzon throughout the early 1970s. In designing an isotropic, spherically shaped, situationally adaptable format for the encoding and decoding of audio - Gerzon's aim was simple; "Areas of music such as 'ambient' music or 'dub offer many new possibilities in how echoes and reverb might be handled in the surround stage, and unexpected innovations in styles of studio production are to be expected in response to ambisonics. " It is this author's view that few technologists and composers have risen to the challenge set by Gerzon. By the non-acceptance of spatial sound, the recording field is not achieving the immersive heights possible for audiences. Progressive methods of delivering music that encapsulates audiences have been publicly available for 30 years and yet the music industry are still constrained by stereo. Using the realism of a

'You are there' experience has been at the heart of music consumption, removing us from our daily lives with joyous reliving of experiences and providing musicologists with the phonograph effect. Despite the spatial audio being central to the current developments within cinema and computer games - consumers are not 'buying' into the technology. Equivalent visual technology has been quick to be implemented, with high definition (HD), high frame rate (HFR), three dimensional visuals (3D) expanding the visual experience. The relationship with our future audible experience has yet to be fully identified - and thus the principle aim of understanding audio-based research and the consumer relationship. Results of this research project have demonstrated the need for a re-examination of the interaction between music and consumers. The reproduction method of sound could be key to removing boundaries between performers and audiences, and yet, there is an indication that the boundary is very much in place.

Keywords

spatial, audio, consumers

Aims

The aims of this presentation is to pursue a discussion into how audio research is perceived by those outside the research. One field, spatial audio, is chosen as a case study because of it's emerging prevalence within media experiences. Methods of audio reproduction have been developed that surpass the current standard (stereophonic) presentation but no data is available as to why such methods have been neglected.

Methods

An internet-based listening test was developed and opened for industry and public responses. The perceptual assessment methodology was an adapted version of the ITU-R BS 1534 scheme. The target responses were from informed listeners, using surround sound systems.

Outcomes

Of the responses - a significant percentage were unable to listen to the surround files due to their lack of appropriate sound systems. A sub-investigation into the failure of spatial audio's acceptance by the audio community then found a lack of suitable, repeatable research. An open debate or discussion could significantly redirect the implementations of immersive audio by considering the views outside of those who research it.

DISCUSSION

The presentation will deliver several key questions, and points of interest, that have been drawn from the research project. These relate to the way that professionals perceive sound reproduction, our evolving method of consumption, and how the wider community view the future of sound technologies.

REFERENCES

Katz, M. (2010), *'Capturing Sound'*, California Press

Søren Bech, Nick Zacharov (2006), *'Perceptual Audio Evaluation - Theory, Method and Application'*, Wiley Press

Horsburgh A. J., Turner, D., Size, J. (2013), 'A Study into the Broadcasting Surround Production Chain', *'Reproduced Sound 2013'*

'The old in the new': teaching and learning traditional music online

▌ Ailbhe Kenny

Mary Immaculate College, Ireland

ABSTRACT

Musical participation online offers a relatively new context for 'musicking' globally. Online music communities, which Salavuo (2006) claims have become "mainstream environments of musical practice" (p. 265), have attracted new research as well as debates in the field of music education. Mansfield (2004) interrogates immersion in this "technoculture" cautioning that musicality should not be lost to new technologies. This presentation examines how the Online Academy of Irish Music (OAIM) functions as a teaching and learning online community for Irish traditional music. Employing a socio-cultural theoretical lens, the online nature of this study sets the context for investigating the teaching and learning of Irish traditional music through the development of a "shared practice" as it is built up through roles and relationships within the online community. Case study research carried out over a nine-month period gathered interactional data from online discussion forums and facebook posts from this online community. Individual perspectives were also sought through participant logs and tutor interviews. The analysis from these multiple data sets offers considerable insights into the OAIM's pedagogy of e-learning, the development of a "shared practice" and the influence of roles and relationships within the community. This presentation reflects a contemporary technological environment for music education and so provides a means to understand and problematise this relatively new form of music teaching and learning.

KEYWORDS

online community, traditonal music, music education

AIMS

Partti and Karlsen (2010) argue that online music communities "challenge music educators to a profound reconsideration of where, how and by what means people become musically educated in this day and age" (p. 379). Through the examination of music teaching and learning within the OAIM this case study aims to capture a unique window into these continually developing online music communities and contribute to the knowledge base to inform new directions in this area of teaching, learning and research.

METHODS

A qualitative instrumental case study approach aimed to gain an in-depth understanding of the teaching and learning processes within the OAIM. Over a nine-month period methods employed included observations of practice from the OAIM website, forums, video tutorials, and Facebook posts. In addition to these collective insights, findings from participant logs and interviews with the tutors offered individual insights into the online case study.

OUTCOMES

Individual and collective insights triangulate from the various data sets to illuminate significant emerging themes and practices in relation to the processes of teaching and learning within the OAIM. Questions are posed regarding the pedagogy of e-learning, the development of a "shared practice" and the influence of roles and relationships within the community. The study found that the OAIM relied heavily on relationships and participation, a maintaining of genre-specific characteristics, and structured pedagogical approaches in order to build a sense of music community amongst teachers and learners and also between the learners themselves. The OAIM represents an emerging approach to Irish traditional music teaching and learning that broadens access globally and facilitates the building of a worldwide online music community.

IMPLICATIONS

The online medium of interaction within the study raises important issues for the growing technological culture of music education. The fact that this music community meets in cyberspace extends the medium for 'musicking' and highlights the importance of extending online music making opportunities. The presentation emphasises the need for music educationalists to seek to understand and continually problematise this relatively new form of musical participation.

REFERENCES

Mansfield, J. E. (2004). The musical subject, technoculture and curriculum in the postmodern condition. *Research Studies in Music Education*, 23(1), 42–58.

Partti, H., & Karlsen, S. (2010). Reconceptualising musical learning: New media, identity and community in music education. *Music Education Research*, 12(4), 369–382.

Salavuo, M. (2006). Open and informal online communities as forums of collaborative musical activities and learning. *British Journal of Music Education*, 23(3), 253–271.

Studio Pedagogy: Perspectives from Producers

▌ Andrew King

University of Hull, UK.

Abstract

This paper considers how educators can develop principles of music production in a digital age. It focuses upon the practice used in the audio industry form both an analogue and digital perspective. Three renowned music producers were interviewed as part of this study. The evaluation of this data involved using Interpretative Phenomenological Analysis (IPA) and revealed: the importance of capturing performance in the studio; the relevance of expertise from a musical and technical perspective; how the affordances of digital technology can affect workflow and decision-making; issues surrounding listening to music and loudness; and the impact of environment and commercial pressures. What is then put forward is a framework for considering designing tasks for students and the foundations for a more in-depth environmental study.

Keywords

recording, studio, decision-making, listening, loudness, capture, performance, workflow, expertise.

Aims

The aim of this study was to explore analogue and digital music production techniques and identify what are the perceived issues in modern music making. By exploring this phenomena form the perspective of three renowned music producers that have worked across both analogue and digital eras of sound recording it is anticipated that a framework for developing teaching music production could be developed.

METHODS

The research design for this study was qualitative in nature and involved in-depth interviews with record producers concerning the use of both analogue and digital technologies in the recording studio. The aims of the study were:

- To understand the phenomenological perspective in the changes between analogue and digital recording methods from an industry perspective; and
- To explore how these changes could potentially impact upon learners engaged with using technology in music production.

For the purposes of this study it was necessary to approach industry professionals with both a wide knowledge of the recording industry and those who have worked during the transition from analogue to digital machinery in the studio. Three renowned experts in the areas of music production, sound engineering, composition and music management were recruited as part of this study:

Chris Kimsey (CK): whose production credits include *The Rolling Stones, Peter Frampton, Marillion, The Cult, Emerson Lake & Palmer, The Chieftains, New Model Army, Duran Duran, Yes, Elton John* and *Paul McCartney;*

Craig Leon (CL): whose production credits include *The Ramones, Blondie, Talking Heads, Méav, Luciano Pavarotti, Andreas Scholl, Sir James Galway, The Pogues, Jesus Jones, The Fall, The Bangles* and *Joshua Bell;* and

Ken Scott (KS): whose production credits include *The Beatles, Elton John, Pink Floyd, Procol Harum, Mahavishnu Orchestra, Duran Duran, The Jeff Beck Group, SuperTramp, Devo, Level 42* and *David Bowie.*

OUTCOMES

The analysis of the producer interviews revealed two super-ordinate themes (Human Perspective, and Knowledge and Skills) each with four separate sub-sections:

- Human perspective: decision-making; artistic touches; environment; and commercial.
- Knowledge and skills: capture of performance; expertise; studio toolsl and workflow.

IMPLICATIONS

The access and affordances that digital technology brings to the young musicians is without doubt a significant enabler for musical creation. Yet how these technologies are harnessed has become an increasingly important consideration for educators. If technology were viewed as a tool involved in the production of music, then an approach that makes the technology more transparent in the process would appear to be fundamental. It would seem the locus of control in some musical genres could too often unnecessarily rest with the technology and those who operate this rather than the artist. This brings to the foreground an important question as to whether the digital technology used to capture human performance in the hands of some users has in some genres changed our perception of music.

REFERENCES

Ballou, G.M. (ed.) 2002: *The Handbook for Sound Engineers*, (Focal Press: Oxford)

Bartlett, B. & Bartlett, J. (2008). *Practical Recording Techniques.* Oxford: Focal Press

Bergh, A. & DeNora, T. (2009). From wind-up to iPod: Technocultures of listening. In N. Cook, E. Clarke, D. Leech-Wilkinson & J. Rink. The Cambridge Companion to *Recorded Music.* New York: Cambridge University Press. 102-115.

Blake, A. (2009). Recording Practices and the Role of the Producer. In N. Cook, E. Clarke, D. Leech-Wilkinson & J. Rink. The Cambridge Companion to *Recorded Music.* New York: Cambridge University Press. 36-53.

Borwick, J. (1996). *Sound Recording Practice.* Oxford: Oxford University Press.

Burgess, R. J. (2008). Producer compensation: Challenges and options in the new music business. *Journal on the Art of Record Production.* 3

Davis, D. & Patronis, E. (2006). *Sound System Engineering.* Oxford: Focal Press.

Firth, S. & Zargorski-Thomas, S. (2012). *The Art of Record Production.* Farnham: Ashgate.

Gillham, B. (2005). *Research Interviewing: The Range of Techniques.* Maidenhead: Open University Press.

Green, L. (2002). *How Popular Musicians Learn: A Way Ahead for Music Education.* Farnham: Ashgate.

Huber, D.M. & Runstein, R.E. (2009). *Modern Recording Techniques.* Oxford: Focal Press.

Katz, M. (2004). *Capturing Sound: How Technology Has Changed Music.* Berkley: University of California Press.

King, A. (2008). Collaborative learning in the music studio. Music Education Research. 10 (3). 423-43.

King, A. (2009). Contingent learning for creative music technologists. *Technology, Pedagogy & Education.* 18 (2). 137-153.

King, A. (2012). The Student Prince: Music-Making with Technology. In G. McPherson & G. Welch (eds.). *The Oxford Handbook of Music Education Volume 2.* New York: Oxford University Press.

Kerstholt, J.H., & Raaijmakers, J.G.W. (1997). Decision making in dynamic task environments. In R. Ranyard, W.R. Crozier & O. Svenson (eds.), *Decision Making: Cognitive Models and Explanations* (pp. 205-217). London: Routledge.

Manning, P. (2013). *Electronic and Computer Music.* Oxford: Oxford University Press.

Moylan, W. (2007). *Understanding and crafting the mix.* Oxford: Focal Press

Mumford, L. (1952). *Art and Technics.* London: Oxford University Press.

Mumford, L. (1967). *The Myth of the Machine.* London: Martin Secker & Warburg Limited.

Norman, D. (1998). *The Design of Everyday Things.* New York: Basic Books.

Pras, A., & Guastivino, C. (2013). The impact of producers' comments and musicians' self-evaluation on perceived recording quality. *Journal of Music, Technology & Education.* 6(1) 81-101.

Pras, A., Lavoie, M., & Guastavino, C. (2013). The impact of technological advances on recording studio practices. *Journal of the*

>   *American Society for Information Science and Technology.* 64(3) 612-626.

Rumsey, F. (2009). Faithful to His Masters Voice? Questions of Fidelity and Infidelity in Music Recording. In Doğantan-Dack, M. *Recorded Music: Philosophical and Critical Reflections.* Middlesex: Middlesex University Press.

Rumsey, F. & McCormick, T. (2009). *Sound and Recording.* Oxford: Focal Press

Slater, M., & Martin, A. (2012). A conceptual foundation for understanding musico-technological creativity. *Journal of Music, Technology & Education.* 5 (1). 59-76.

Smith, J.A., Flowers, P. & Larkin, M. (2009). *Interpretative Phenomenological Analysis.* London: Sage.

Taylor, T. D. (2001). *Strange Sounds: Music, Technology & Culture.* New York: Routledge.

Théberge, P. (1997). *Any Sound You Can Imagine: Making Music/Consuming Technology.* Hanover: Wesleyan University Press.

Théberge, P. (2012). The End of the World as We Know It: The Changing Role of the Studio in the Age of the Internet. In S. Frith & S. Zargorski-Thomas (eds.), *The Art of Record Production* (pp. 77-90). Farnham: Ashgate.

Vickers, E. (2010). The Loudness War: Background Speculation and Recommendations (pp. 1-27). In *The Proceedings of the Audio Engineering Society 129th Convention.* San Francisco: USA

Introducing technology in Cypriot primary classroom music lessons: "I learnt using things in music I didn't know existed"

▌ Chrysovalentini Konstantinou

University of Cambridge, PhD student, United Kingdom

Abstract

This presentation will address issues around the use and introduction of technology in primary music education with particular reference to a study set in Cyprus which looks at the change in teachers' practices, thinking and concerns as they become more engaged with technology and use it more. The focus of this presentation is the availability and use of technology in music lessons, the creative thinking and teaching with technology and the elements that facilitate the introduction and use of technology in music lessons. The study examines the cases of 10 primary music teachers in Cyprus and uses interviews, questionnaires, observations and teacher reflection. It was indicated that if encouraged and provided with the technology, education, support and training they need, can overcome their hesitations and use technology in their lessons.

Keywords

technology, music education, primary

Aims

Technological developments and changes in education, and specifically music education, are rapid and enormous. Students have enormous possibilities in music using technology accessible to them, ranging from composing with computers, keyboards, mobile technology, to learning and practicing on music concepts through software programs and online activities. Teachers need to find the ways to introduce technology in their music lessons; and during this effort their concerns, views and practices change along with the technology they choose to use and the level of use. Recently new curriculum documents have been developed in Cyprus as part of the educational reform. The new music curriculum documents encourage the use of technology in music lessons. An appendix accompanies the new document which is dedicated to music technology and includes information and suggestions for the teachers. The new curriculum documents, and particularly this study, invited the participants to introduce technology in their music lessons. As teachers started using technology their concerns, views, thinking and practices were changing at the same time. Various models have been developed to assess individuals' progress and change when adopting new methods and technologies. One of these is the Concerns-Based Adoption Model (CBAM). The Concerns-Based Adoption Model (CBAM) is a model which examines individuals' concerns when an innovation (i.e. the introduction of technology in music lessons) is introduced. Concerns are the 'feelings, preoccupation, thought and consideration given to a particular issue or task' (Hall, George and Rutherford, 1978, p.4).

Methods

The methodology followed is a combination of case study approach and action research. Aspects of both can be identified in the research design. Particularly, the cases of 10 teachers who are following action research reflecting cycles are examined. Three stages comprise the research design of this study including various methods. The research design was influenced by the CBAM model and some of the model's tools were used and adjusted. The first stage aimed to provide information regarding the participants' knowledge, use of technology, concerns and thinking on the introduction of technology in music lessons at the beginning of the data collection period. It involved teachers' and students' questionnaires and individual interview with the teachers along with 'acclimatization' observations were possible. The main part of the study, the second stage, consisted mainly of the reflective cycles while the third stage was similar to the first stage and had mainly an evaluative nature. The second stage's cycles are considered reflective as the driving force is teachers' reflections on the introduction and use of technology in music lessons. The reflective cycles involve group meetings, reflective diaries and interviews, collecting students' compositions and teaching and observing lessons. The collected data aimed to examine teachers' change through the cycles and compare their final views, concerns and practices to those recorded in the first stage.

OUTCOMES

Cypriot schools are generally equipped with technology by the Ministry of Education and Culture (MOEC) which depending from the school can vary between computer(s), projector, IWB, keyboard, speakers, and a computer room. Also, different software programs can be found. Teachers during the study used the technology they had available such as computers, IWBs, projectors, electronic piano, CD-players, laptops and a variety of software programs and websites. Some kinds of technology were used more often than others. Various reasons influenced teachers' selections like the technology's availability, students' age, lesson's aims and teacher's skills and knowledge. Technology was used differently by the teachers and some software programs were preferred than others. They might be using the same program but in different ways because of the students' age and their knowledge and skills. The programs used more often were the *Emelia* and the listening maps which were easier to use and introduce and did not require as musical or technological expertise as other programs. Also, when teachers became more familiar and comfortable with technology, they started thinking more creatively and using the resources in more creative ways. Most students involved in the study were given the opportunity to use technology themselves either during whole-class activities or in small groups to practice music concepts or compose. Students' excitement, engagement and motivation when using technology was more than evident during the lessons and relevant comments were recorded in their questionnaires.

IMPLICATIONS AND DISCUSSION

For the technology to be effectively introduced by teachers, training seminars and resources are essential, as this study indicated. Other facilitating elements in the effort of introducing technology in music lessons are the support provided and the availability of technology. Taking into account teachers' needs and these facilitating elements is one of the first steps to take for an effective and sustainable introduction and use of technology in music lessons. Even though the study was focused in Cypriot primary teachers, other music educators who are expected to use technology in their music lessons and may be in similar position as Cypriot educators can be encouraged and inspired.

ACKNOWLEDGEMENTS

The present study is part of my PhD, supervised by Dr Pamela Burnard and Dr Linda Hargreaves.

REFERENCES

Hall, G. E., George, A. A. and Rutherford, W. L. (1978). *Stages of concern about the innovation: the concept, verification, and implications.* University of Texas. Research and Development Center for Teacher Education.

The EARS 2 Pedagogical Project – an eLearning environment to introduce learners to sound-based music

❙ Leigh Landy

    De Montfort University, United Kingdom

❙ Sarah Younie

    De Montfort University, United Kingdom

❙ Andrew Hill

    De Montfort University, United Kingdom

❙ Motje Wolf

    De Montfort University, United Kingdom

Abstract

Discussions have been on-going in the UK regarding how to offer the broadest musical repertoire possible to young learners be it with some opposition. At the MTI Research Centre, we have been dealing with the issue of experimental music and access for almost 15 years discovering, for example, that a large portion of young learners (in some cases, the majority) are open to music made with sounds and not just notes. As a consequence of 1) the desire to make innovative music accessible to young people, the educational rationale to address both enhanced listening and creativity, in our case with sounds, and 2) Unesco's suggestion that the MTI consider offering an ElectroAcoustic Resource Site (EARS, www.ears.dmu.ac.uk) for children, the idea of the EARS 2 pedagogical project was born. The goal of EARS 2 is to achieve a user-friendly eLearning environment intended to introduce relevant aspects of electroacoustic (or sound-based) music to young learners. The *paper* will present the entire project including the EARS 2 eLearning environment, its vision, its key characteristics and its means of operation alongside that of its creative software platform, Compose with Sounds

(CwS) that was funded by the EU and tested in schools in six European countries. EARS 2 will be not only translated, but also culturally conditioned for use in countries beyond the UK; thus, our international vision will also be presented. Sarah Younie will present its innovative aspects from an educational studies point of view. This will include remarks concerning methodological issues. The paper will conclude with a summary of future plans related to both the eLearning site and the creative software platform. The associated *workshop* will offer hands-on experience regarding both the eLearning site and creative software and include an introduction to the teachers' packs to all interested parties at the Sempre conference.

KEYWORDS

Electroacoustic Music, eLearning, KS2 & 3

AIMS

To achieve a user-friendly eLearning environment, EARS 2, originally focussed on KS3 students (but now identified as of use to the latter years of KS2 as well), intends to introduce relevant aspects to electroacoustic or sound-based music to young learners. The site is directly linked with the website of its creative software environment, Compose with Sounds (CwS) that was separately funded and developed slightly earlier. CwS can be used independently as can EARS 2 and has been made to be as intuitive as possible to new users; both are open to interested people of all ages, not only students within class groups. The site offers multiple forms of navigation from linear progression following its three learning levels (reflecting the three years of KS3; CwS also contains three levels of functions reflecting the EARS 2 levels) to thematic navigation to an *à la carte* experience. It works on multiple platforms and the only requirement for EARS 2/CwS is a computer and an Internet connection. It is concept driven (e.g., real-world and abstract sounds); this means that all aspects of a relevant concept are introduced simultaneously, e.g., musical, historical, theoretical, technological, extra-musical, repertoire and creative application. The three main headers on the site are: create, learn and listen. In time it will be available in a significant number of languages whereby the site will not only be translated, but also 'culturally conditioned' for particular learning approaches and using examples relevant to the language area. Furthermore, EARS 2 will offer social tools allowing for communities of interest to form in this area of experimenting with sound.

METHODS

For the project, the online environment was pedagogically informed using a constructivist approach to learning, which has at its heart discovery or inquiry-based learning. Rather than offering one linear learning path, the online environment allows learners to explore sound-based music in a learner centred way, with a variety of learning activities that both support and challenge the learner. The EARS2 site is pedagogically framed by an active learning approach, which enables the learner to engage in information acquisition and the active demonstration of learned concepts.

The pedagogic principles on which the project was founded relate to those theories of learning which pertain to social constructivism and distributed cognition. Social constructivism as developed by the Soviet psychologist Vygotsky (1986) asserts that learning is embedded within interactions, which include interactions with objects, people and events in the environment. Vygotsky (1986) argued that the development of higher mental functions is mediated by signs and sign systems. With technology as a sign system, the online environment becomes a key mediator in the learning process. Hence the technology fundamentally contributes to and enhances the learning process.

Distributed cognition is a psychological theory of learning which argues that 'cognitive activity is constructed both from internal and external resources, and the meaning of our actions is grounded in the context of the activity' (Hollan et al. 2000 p.179). A key tenant of the theory is that knowledge does not only lie within the individual, but also in the individual's social and physical environment. It builds upon social constructivism and extends it to 'technology' and computed mediated interactions.

OUTCOMES

The specific outcomes are the creative software, Compose with Sounds and its hosting website, cws.dmu.ac.uk as well as the EARS 2 pedagogical eLearning environment hosted at www.ears2.dmu.ac.uk (in development). Beyond this, there are the project's teachers' packs (by Motje Wolf) and a number of associated publications, not least Landy's latest book, "Making Music with Sounds".

IMPLICATIONS

As we have already discovered, due to the PhD work of Nasia Therapontos supervised by the first two presenters, this approach can have significant implications. The Cyprus Ministry of Education is considering implementing her approach to learning in electroacoustic music for the age group 9-14 as part of their new national curriculum. If this were to succeed EARS 2's Greek version would form an integral part of this curriculum. By way of the team's negotiating with regional and national organisations, it is our hope that schools around the UK and abroad will consider its use for the introduction of electroacoustic music or as a significant aspect of the introduction of music technology in general.

ACKNOWLEDGEMENTS

EU Culture 2007 programme, HEIF5 funds

REFERENCES

Hollan, J., Hutchins, E., Kirsh, D. (2000). Distributed Cognition: Toward A New Foundation For Human Computer Interaction Research. San Diego: University of California. *ACM Transcriptions on Computer Human Interaction*, 7 (2), 174-196.

Landy, L. (2012). *Making Music with Sounds*. NY: Routledge

Landy, L., Hall, R., Uwins, M. (2013). "Widening Participation in Electroacoustic Music: The EARS 2 pedagogical initiatives".

Therapontos, N. (2013) *Evolving Music Education in the Digital Age. Sound-based music in public schools of Cyprus*. De Montfort University: PhD Thesis.

Vygotsky, L. (1986) *Thought and language*. Cambridge, MA: The MIT Press.

Wolf, M. (2013a). "The Appreciation of Electroacoustic Music: The prototype of the pedagogical ElectroAcoustic Resource Site". *Organised Sound, 18/2*, {108–123; 124-133}.

Wolf, M. (2013b) *The Appreciation of Electroacoustic Music – An Empirical Study with Inexperienced Listeners*, De Montfort University: PhD thesis. Available from: http://tinyurl.com/o2o4kd3

Younie, S. and Leask, M. (2013) Teaching with Technologies: The Essential Guide, Buckingham: Open University Press.

FourChords Guitar Karaoke Makes Learning Guitar Easy

Paula Lehto
CMO, Finland

Abstract

FourChords Guitar Karaoke with easy chords and lyrics makes learning to play new songs with a guitar much easier than in the traditional ways. It can be used individually or in the classrooms.

Keywords

music education, guitar, mobile app

Aims

Mobile applications can be used to help students to learn to play Instruments the easy way. Teacher can work with groups where some students are playing, some are singing and some are making the rhythm.. FourChords app is available for iPhone and iPad and can be shown in the TV-screen too. Sessions can be recorded and shared.

Methods

In the FourChords App the songs are re-arranged into easy versions that can be played only with a few open chords. The karaoke-style display with a backing track helps to play chords at the right time. FourChords keeps students motivated and makes playing and singing in groups easy.

OUTCOMES

More students can learn to play songs with the guitar and they have fun making music together. Students stay motivated to learn more about playing and music theory once they have an experience of playing the music they like = making music. More engaged students.

TECHNOLOGY CAN HELP PEOPLE TO LEARN MUSIC AND EXPERIENCE MUSIC.

Over half of the people that start to play on instument quit before they reach on enjoyable skill level. With new technology we can improve the situation and make the learning easier and more fun.

Ecocompositional techniques in ubiquitous music practices in educational settings: Sonic sketching

▌ Maria Helena de Lima
   Federal University of Rio Grande do Sul - UFRGS, Brazil

▌ Damián Keller
   Federal University of Acre - UFAC, Brazil

▌ Nuno Otero
   Linnaeus University, Sweden

▌ Marcelo Soares Pimenta
   Federal University of Rio Grande do Sul - UFRGS, Brazil

▌ Victor Lazzarini
   Naional University of Ireland, Maynooth, Ireland

▌ Marcelo Johann
   Federal University of Rio Grande do Sul - UFRGS, Brazil

▌ Leandro Costalonga
   Federal University of Espirito Santo - UFES Brazil

ABSTRACT

We present results of the application of ecocompositional techniques in formal musical learning contexts. Two exploratory studies were conducted to assess the effectiveness of sonic sketching support tools for ubiquitous musical activities: 1. one involving high-school students at an introductory ubiquitous music course taught at the Application College, UFRGS; 2. another targeting undergraduate students doing regular course work on creative musical practices at NAP - Amazon Music Research Center, UFAC. All activities were undertaken within a four-month period with one-per-week group sessions and continuous on-line exchanges. Sonic sketching techniques were developed and tested through a participatory design approach featuring iterative cycles of proposals, applications and critiques. The creative yield of the two studies featured three musical products published in artistic venues. We discuss the limitations of the current technological support for early stage creative decision making and propose sonic sketching strategies to enable musicking within and beyond formal learning environments. Musical and audiovisual examples are included in the presentation.

KEYWORDS

ubiquitous music, graphic-procedimental tagging, sonic sketching

AIMS

Sonic sketching: Musical creativity has received increased attention both from domain-specific perspectives (Burnard, 2012; Collins, 2012; Keller et al., 2013; Odena, 2012) and from general creativity studies (Sawyer, 2006). Despite recent advances in technological development for musical interaction (Holland et al., 2013), support for creativity-centered musical interaction design remains elusive (Coughlan and Johnson, 2006; Liikkanen et al., 2011; Lima et al., 2012). A particularly difficult problem in this area is how to integrate everyday settings and materials within musicking practices (Small, 1998) without constraining the creative potential of the participants (DiLiello and Houghton, 2008; Runco, 1994). This area of research - termed everyday musical creativity - is one of the central topics being pursued in Ubiquitous Music research (Keller et al., 2011a). A growing number of ecocompositional techniques (Keller and Capasso, 2006) provide support for creative decisions in the early stages of ubiquitous musical creative cycles, including the planning, design of creative products (Lima et al., 2012). We propose sonic sketching as a term to encompass these techniques. Two case studies are presented. The first study applies sonic sketching as a cumulative decision-making procedure. The second study comprises two cases that use audiovisual scores as tools to anchor sonic activity (Keller et al., 2010). The first case combines the ecocompositional technique proposed by Nance (2007) - the aural score - with a new interaction metaphor: graphic-procedimental tagging (Melo, 2013; Melo and Keller, 2013). The second case features graphic-procedimental tagging as a tool to support group improvisatory vocal activities by musically untrained participants (Mesquita, 2013). The technological infra-structure includes consumer-level mobile telephones for SMS text exchanges and compressed video footage for time-based visual instructions.

Methods

Study 1: sonic sketching as cumulative creative decision making Fourteen high-school students participated in the recently created introductory music technology elective class: Ubiquitous Music at CAp (Application College, UFRGS) (Lima, 2013). All students had previous curricular music o informal musical trainning, including vocal or instrumental music practice. None of the students had formal training in IT (information technology), but all of the participants had used IT in musical informal activities. The Ubiquitous Music Planning protocol (Lima et al., 2012) was applied to select activities, materials and tools. The support tools included Facebook and Skype. Two sonic tools were adopted: the cooperative compositional environment CODES (Miletto et al., 2011) and the shareware sound editor Kristal (www.kreatives.org/kristal/). Students worked in groups involving dialogical exchanges of proposals and critiques, doing co-located collaborative one-per-week class sessions, during a period of four months. One student adopted ecocompositional techniques for her found-sound mixing project. She applied sonic sketching as a cumulative decision-making procedure. Sonic choices determined asynchronous creative decisions through a cycle of constrain/expand /shift operations (Keller, 2012). The result was a sonic work in which the events of the initial materials provided the temporal anchors that supported the decisions for the new mix. All groups completed their projects and presented results in class and on-line. They also participated and discussed their projects with ubiquitous music researchers in an informal session during the IV Workshop on Ubiquitous Music (IV UbiMus 2013, Porto Alegre, Brazil). Study 2: graphic-procedimental tagging During a four-month period, seven music undergraduate students group took part in regular course work on creative musical practice at the Amazon Center for Music Research (NAP). Activities included one-per-week group sessions and continuous on-line exchanges. The students could freely choose their tools and materials depending on the demands of each project. The groups explored the application of various sonic sketching techniques, including video prototyping (Mackay and Fayard, 1999), vocal sketching (Ekman and Rinott, 2010), time tagging (Keller et al., 2010), and spatial tagging (Keller et al., 2011b). An interaction technique involving the use of photographs and video footage, inspired in the tradition of the experimental-music graphic scores was devised: graphic-procedimental tagging (Melo and Keller 2013). Location-specific visual material is anchored (Keller et al., 2010) through a bidimensional reference system. The visual anchors correspond to time-based events that are used as performance instructions within an audiovisual score. Two students worked on independent projects that incorporated graphic-procedimental tagging within their musicking activities. One project targeted musicians, yielding a mixed media work for two clarinetists and a video score with a soundscape audiotrack. Another project involved fifteen untrained participants in a vocal improvisatory performance that used portable devices to send instructions. Both works were presented during the International Symposium on Music in the Amazon (SIMA 2013, Rio Branco, Brazil).

OUTCOMES

Sketching (Buxton, 2007) has proven to be an effective strategy for designing visual and tangible elements of interactive systems. Through a participatory design approach, involving iterative cycles of proposals, applications and critiques, both high-school and university students with various backgrounds managed to obtain creative musical results within a four-month period of activity. The three examples discussed indicate that sonic sketching techniques may be useful for cumulative decision making, mixed media synchronous musical activities and group co-located improvisatory practices in educational contexts using a collaborative technological everyday tools.

OUTCOMES AND IMPLICATIONS

Sketching (Buxton, 2007) has proven to be an effective strategy for designing visual and tangible elements of interactive systems. Through a participatory design approach, involving iterative cycles of proposals, applications and critiques, both high-school and university students with various backgrounds managed to obtain creative musical results within a four-month period of activity. The three examples discussed indicate that sonic sketching techniques may be useful for cumulative decision making, mixed media synchronous musical activities and group co-located improvisatory practices in educational contexts using a collaborative technological everyday tools.

ACKNOWLEDGEMENTS

CNPq, CAPES, CAp-UFRGS.

REFERENCES

Burnard, P. (2012). *Musical Creativities in Real World Practice*. Oxford, UK: Oxford University Press. (ISBN: 9780199583942.)

Keller, D. (2012). Sonic Ecologies. In A. R. Brown (ed.), *Sound Musicianship: Understanding the Crafts of Music* (pp. 213-

227). Newcastle upon Tyne, UK: Cambridge Scholars Publishing. (ISBN: 978-1-4438-3912-9.)

Lima, M. H., Keller, D., Pimenta, M. S., Lazzarini, V. & Miletto, E. M. (2012). Creativity-centred design for ubiquitous musical activities: Two case studies. *Journal of Music, Technology and Education* 5 (2), 195-222. (Doi: 10.1386/jmte.5.2.195_1.)

BIBLIOGRAPHY

Buxton, W. (2007). *Sketching User Experiences: Getting the Design Right and the Right Design.* New York, NY: Elsevier / Morgan Kaufmann. (ISBN: 9780123740373.)

Collins, D. (2012). 'Getting there': Do we need to study how people compose music?. *Journal of Music, Technology and Education 4* (2-3), 170-173.

Coughlan, T. & Johnson, P. (2006). Interaction in creative tasks. In *Proceedings of the SIGCHI Conference on Human Factors in Computing Systems* (pp. 531-540). ACM. (ISBN: 1-59593-372-7.)

DiLiello, T. C. & Houghton, J. D. (2008). Creative potential and practised creativity: Identifying untapped creativity in organizations. *Creativity and Innovation Management 17* (1), 37-46. (Doi: 10.1111/j.1467-8691.2007.00464.x.)

Ekman, I. & Rinott, M. (2010). Using vocal sketching for designing sonic interactions. In *Proceedings of the 8th ACM Conference on Designing Interactive Systems (DIS '10)* (pp. 123-131). New York, NY: ACM. (ISBN: 978-1-4503-0103-9.)

Holland, S., Wilkie, K., Mulholland, P. & Seago, A., (eds.) (2013). *Music and Human-Computer Interaction.* London, UK: Springer. (ISBN: 9781447129905.)

Keller, D., Ferreira da Silva, E., Pinheiro da Silva, F., Lima, M. H., Pimenta, M. S. & Lazzarini, V. (2013). Criatividade musical cotidiana: Um estudo exploratório com sons vocais percussivos. In *Anais do Congresso da Associação Nacional de Pesquisa e Pós-Graduação em Música - ANPPOM.* Natal, RN: ANPPOM.

Keller, D., Flores, L. V., Pimenta, M. S., Capasso, A. & Tinajero, P. (2011a). Convergent trends toward ubiquitous music. *Journal of New Music Research 40* (3), 265-276.

Efficient Computer-Aided Pitch Track and Note Estimation for Scientific Applications

▌ Matthias Mauch

    Centre for Digital Music, Queen Mary University of London, UK

▌ Chris Cannam

    Centre for Digital Music, Queen Mary University of London, UK

▌ György Fazekas

    Centre for Digital Music, Queen Mary University of London, UK

ABSTRACT

We present *Tony*, a free, open-source software tool for computer-aided pitch track and note annotation of melodic audio content. The accurate annotation of fundamental frequencies and notes is essential to the scientific study of intonation in singing and other instruments. Unlike commercial applications for singers and producers or other academic tools for generic music annotation and visualisation *Tony* has been designed for the scientific study of monophonic music: a) it implements state-of-the art algorithms for pitch and note estimation from audio, b) it provides visual and auditory feedback of the extracted pitches for the identification of detection errors, c) it provides an intelligent graphical user interface through which the user can identify and rapidly correct estimation errors, d) it provides functions for exporting pitch track and note track enabling further processing in spreadsheets or other applications. Software versions for Windows, OSX and Linux platforms can be downloaded from http://code.soundsoftware.ac.uk/projects/tony

KEYWORDS

Pitch/Note Analysis, Software, Singing

AIMS

Our goal is to make the annotation of melodic content for scientific analysis more efficient. Music psychologists interested in the analysis of pitch and intonation usually use software programs originally aimed at the analysis of speech (e.g. Praat www.fon.hum.uva.nl/praat/) or generic audio annotation tools (e.g. Sonic Visualiser www.sonicvisualiser.org) to extract pitches of notes from audio recordings. Since these programs were not conceived for musical pitch analysis, the process of extracting note frequencies remains laborious and can take many times the duration of the recording. Commercial tools such as Melodyne (www.celemony.com/), Songs2See (www.songs2see.com/) or Sing&See (www.singandsee.com/) also exists for these purposes. However, their frequency estimation procedures are typically not public (proprietary code), and they do not provide export formats well suited for scientific analysis. A pitch annotation system [1] developed for scientific use exists, but it does not feature note extraction, and it is not available as free and open-source software. This is why, during research on intonation [2], we decided to develop our own tool that would avoid the above shortcomings.

METHODS

For automatic pitch and note estimation we use the pYIN method [3]. The method provides precise pitch and note estimates and automatically determines which parts of the recording are voiced. The graphical user interface is based upon open source software libraries originally developed for the Sonic Visualiser software. It shows the audio waveform, a spectrogram representation, the pitch track and notes. Users can scroll and zoom in time. *Tony* does not only play back the original audio, but also, optionally, sonifications of the pitch track (melody line) and the note track (discrete pitches with durations). Notes' pitches are estimated using the median of the pitch track corresponding to the time extent (duration) of the note. The user can delete, move, cut, merge, crop and extend notes, and the notes' frequency is adapted accordingly. The user can delete spurious parts of the pitch track and shift the pitch track in frequency. In order to efficiently correct erroneous pitch tracks, the user can select a time interval, and *Tony* will provide various alternative pitch tracks. The user can then pick the correct one.

OUTCOMES

The system is currently used for two projects: 1) the generation of new training and test data for Music Informatics research, and 2) a research project on intonation in unaccompanied solo singing. Preliminary feedback by the users suggests that the system does indeed facilitate pitch annotation and provides vital features that cannot be found in other tools.

Conclusions

We presented *Tony*, a new software tool for computer-assisted annotation of melodic audio content for scientific analysis. No other existing program combines pitch and note estimation, a graphical user interface with auditory feedback, rapid, computer-aided correction of pitches and extensive exporting facilities. *Tony* is freely available for use on Windows, OSX and Linux platforms from

http://code.soundsoftware.ac.uk/projects/tony/.

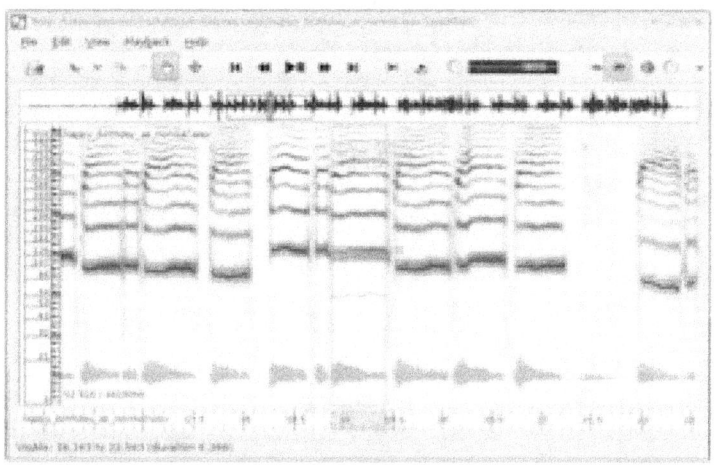

Acknowledgements

Matthias Mauch is funded by the Royal Academy of Engineering. We would like to thank Justin Salamon, Rachel Bittner and Juan Bello for their comments and coding help.

References

Pant, S., Rao, V., & Rao, P. (2010). A melody detection user interface for polyphonic music. *2010 National Conference On Communications (NCC)*, 2010.

Mauch, M., Frieler, K., & Dixon, S. (under review). *Intonation in Unaccompanied Singing: Accuracy, Drift and a Model of Intonation Memory.*

Mauch, M., & Dixon, S. (2014). pYIN : a Fundamental Frequency Estimator Using Probabilistic Threshold Distributions. In *Proceedings of the IEEE International Conference on Acoustics, Speech and Signal Processing (ICASSP 2014).*

Vygotsky, Eliot, and Linguistic Crossroads: Transposing Musical Beauty for the Language Classroom

▌ Andrew Meyerhoff

Saga University, Japan

Abstract

An age-old adage maintains "beauty is in the eyes of the beholder". Similarly, this axiom can be transposed to music: beauty is in the ears of the listener. Thus, what is beauty? The obvious answer is beauty varies from person to person. If applying Vygostky (1978) to music education, listeners lean towards musical forms which lie within their comfort zones, yet lose interest if music is too predictable. According to Zones of Proximal Development (ZPD) learning is extended out from concentric rings: the inner ring being what students know and can do comfortably, the middle ring is what they are familiar with but cannot yet apply, and the outer ring being the zone beyond their present knowledge and ability. Therefore, it is the challenge of the educator to target learning in the middle ring, with movement toward the outer. For an ESL instructor using songs in the language classroom, ZPDs become especially problematic due to overlapping ZPDs such as culture, age, and gender. Another factor Murphey and Alber (1985) note is contemporariness. These two researchers suggest that songs for language learning are only useful if they are contemporary. This make senses as contemporariness brings songs into a closer ZPD. Obviously, songs provide a context for learning. However, if songs are out of students' ZPD, using songs for language learning would be futile. Unfortunately, many language instructors naively impose their own aesthetic values on students when selecting songs. In contrast to the aesthetic view, Eliot (1995) suggests that music listening involves information specific to culture, and, as a result, music listening is not a universal experience. Dogma that music can be judged objectively is both too prescriptive and restrictive. With this fallacy in mind, the author sought to answer the following question: How can ESL instructors investigate students' tastes and perceived needs to choose songs that best fit different cultural contexts? The following paper details the results of a study conducted over two semesters with freshmen university students in Fall of 2012 and Spring of 2013. Fifteen questions, including open-ended and close-ended components, were asked. Questions included factors such as singer's stance, likeability, memorability, and perceived usefulness for language learning. The Fall 2012 study focused on only contemporary English songs chosen from Tokyo Inter-FM's top 100 charts, whereas the Spring 2013 study had students listening to a cross-section of songs over the past three decades. The author adapted a greater cross-section in the second semester to analyse for variance between contemporary songs and older songs. The study concludes by showing how results concur with a praxis-based curriculum involving music grounded in a specific cultural context (Eliot, ibid. p. 14): Japanese first year university ESL students in their own culture. Truly, beauty does lie in the ears of the listener, and as such language, instructors must take off their cultural earplugs and tune into their students' needs.

KEYWORDS

ESL, Zones of Proximal Development (ZPD), Praxis-based approach

AIMS

To discern to what degree ZPDs play upon student likeability and perceived usefulness of English songs in the ESL classroom, and how instructors can incorporate this information to make better song selections for students that scaffold from familiar to unfamiliar, and relatively simple to complex.

METHODS

The author used a grounded theory approach in order to find emerging patterns. A 15 question survey was given for each song with each question having both an open-ended and closed-ended component. The sample population consisted of 15 students in semester one, and 49 students in semester two, with an almost even split in gender. Six students were randomly highlighted from each semester to look at patterns emerging from anecdotal comments, but the quantitative data was derived from all students. An equal number of songs sung by males and females were used, as well as a balance between pop and rock songs. The first semester utilized only contemporary songs, whereas the second semester added older songs, as well; to test for the impact of contemporariness.

OUTCOMES

Results showed Japanese students favoured foreign songs containing traits found in Japanese songs. As could be expected, males preferred rock music and songs sung by males, whereas females liked pop songs and songs sung by females. Perhaps the greatest phenomenon found in the data is that students liked songs in which they agreed with the singer's stance. A few songs were generally disliked; they were perceived as expressing culturally undesirable traits such as selfishness, and conceit. In hindsight, this might be expected as humility and social conformity are greatly admired attributes in Japanese culture. Lastly, Murphey and Albers' contention that only contemporary songs are useful for the language classroom is only partly true as one contemporary song was largely disliked, whereas a few older songs were liked by all. It would appear that "stance" acted in strong competition with contemporariness for these songs; thus, one substantial finding made in this study was the role of "stance" when applying a praxis-based approach to the use of songs in the ESL classroom.

IMPLICATIONS

Clearly, as suggested earlier, beauty lies in the ears of the listener. Through such types of research, we can gain greater insight into students' ZPDs, and make better song selections for the classroom. However, as this research was limited in scope and scale, it is suggested that follow up studies are conducted in the future, especially looking at cross-cultural studies of language students from various cultures, to discern how beauty is beheld in these cultures, too.

REFERENCES

Eliot, David J. (1995). Music Matters: *A new philosophy of music education*. Oxford, UK: Oxford University Press.

Murphey, T. & Alber, J. (1985). A Pop Song Register: The motherese of adolescencts as affective foreign talk. *TESOL Quarterly*, 19 (4), 793-795.

Vygostky, Lev (1978). *Minds and Society: The development of higher psychological processes*. Cambridge, MA: Harvard University Press.

How pianists listen to recordings of Schumann's Träumerei?: Comparisons with self-evaluation and external-evaluation

▌ Yuki Morijiri

Institute of Education, University of London, UK

ABSTRACT

This research aimed to investigate how pianists evaluate (a) their own performances and (b) performances by other pianists, and also how these constructions of criteria might be related. Six professional pianists took part in the research, including recording sessions using Schumann's Träumerai, with self-evaluation and external-evaluation using six recordings of each. A triadic method from a Repertory grid technique was used as a method and, as a result, grids for both contents and structures were elicited as personal constructs from each performer. The results revealed that the criteria used to evaluate performances were mainly tone quality, pedalling, phrasing, tempo and overall musical expression. In addition, criteria for self-evaluation and for external-evaluation highly overlapped for each performer. It could be said that pianists use similar criteria when evaluating their own performances and also the performances of other pianists.

KEYWORDS

piano performance, criteria, triadic method

AIMS

The aim of this research study was to investigate the construction of performance criteria by pianists and how such criteria were applied regarding both their own performances and the performance of other pianists in Western classical music.

METHODS

Participants were six professional pianists (Male = 3, Female = 3) based in the UK. The mean age of the participants was 31.5 years old. They were asked to record six performances each of Schumann's Träumerai in a hired hall with a YAMAHA grand piano. Within two months after recordings, each of the participants came to a laboratory and listened to, evaluated and made comparison between their own six recordings, using a Triadic method (cf. Fransella, Bell & Banniser, 2004; Wapnick, Flowers, Alegant & Jsinskas, 1993). The participants ranked their six performances and chose the best one (cf. Thompson, Diamon & Balkwill, 1998). Within two months after this self-evaluation, the participants returned to the laboratory and evaluated a further six recordings (made up of the 'best'), which included the adjudicator's own best recording (but this is not informed). The participants ranked the performances and chose the best performance amongst these six. Analyses were undertaken, based on a repertory grid technique and revealed clusters in terms of each performance and also the structuring of evaluation criteria.

OUTCOMES

The average length of each performance was 2:35 minutes (range 2:03 – 3.33 mins). The results of a repeated measures analysis of variance (ANOVA) showed a significant difference in terms of each performer's mean time duration in performing the piece, $F (5, 25)=4.06$, $p= .008$, $\_p2= .45$. This result indicated that strong individual differences in performers' perceptions of the music, even though all of performers played the same piece of music. In self-evaluation, performers were likely to choose their best performance from the 5th or 6th trial of their six recordings. The criteria that performers used to evaluate performances were mainly the elements related to tone quality, phrasing, pedalling, tempi and overall musical expression, such as story telling and having a 'dream character'. For the same pianists' ratings as judges for an external evaluation of six 'best' pieces overall, the rankings of each performance were subjected to a repeated measures ANOVA. This analysis revealed a significant main effect of performance: $F (5, 25) = 7.02$, $P<.001$, $\_p2= .58$. Performer F was chosen as having the best performance overall and Performer D was ranked as the lowest. 83.3% of the performers were able to identify to their own recording amongst the six used in the external evaluation session, having been informed at the end of the blind judging session that one of recordings was their own one subsequently. According to their own reports, the reasons why they could identify their own recordings were mainly related to tone quality, phrasing and dynamics. The criteria used in this external evaluations included tone quality, phrasing, pedalling, tempi and overall musical expression, as well as self-evaluation. Also the criteria for self-evaluation and for in external-evaluation highly overlapped for each performer (Kendall Coefficient of Concordance, w=.746, p<.001). It could be said that pianists in this research have similar constructs of criteria for the evaluation of piano performances, whether by themselves or by other pianists.

ACKNOWLEDGEMENTS

This research project has been supported by Sempre award. I would like to express my gratitude to SEMRE for its financial support, to Professor Graham Welch for his guidance and encouragement and to the six pianists for their participation in this research.

REFERENCES

Fransella, F., Bell, R., & Bannister, D. (2004). *A manual for repertory grid technique*. 2nd edition. West Sussex, UK: John Wiley & Sons Ltd.

Thompson, W. F., Diamond, C. T. P., & Balkwill, L. (1998). The adjudication of six performances of a Chopin etude: a study of expert knowledge. *Psychology of music*, 26, 154-174.

Wapnick, J., Flowers, P., Alegant, M., & Jasinskas, L. (1993). *Consistency in piano performance evaluation*. Journal of Research in Music Education, 41(4), 282-292.

"I can do it!": Using the iPad in musical performance with students with special needs

‖ Clint Randles

University of South Florida, United States

ABSTRACT

Purpose: The purpose of this session is to report on some ongoing research on the use of the iPad as a musical instrument for high school students with special needs (Cerebral Palsy, Autism, and Down Syndrome). Multiple techniques were employed under the umbrella of a multiple case study. Research suggests that the most cited criterion for being a "good musician" among high school students is being able to play an instrument (Randles, 2011). However, musical instruments require a great deal of technical facility, which is to some extent unachievable by many special needs students. The work of Tod Machover and the MIT Media Lab has helped the general population realize how technology can unlock musical creativity for students who might be limited by some physical and/or cognitive limitation (www.youtube.com/watch?v=Zj2QoLhfwew). This session reports on the exploration of what the motion sensitive component of the iPad (the specific app Cosmovox), and conventional (Garageband) and non-conventional (ThumbJam) graphic interfaces might mean for this population. The creative processes of research participants and the role of music as a meaning making enterprise have been examined, among other phenomena. The population for this study is a class that meets weekly in the Psychiatry building on the USF Tampa campus. The class is sponsored by VSA Florida (housed at the University of South Florida), the state branch of VSA, the International Organization on Arts and Disability, a program of the Kennedy Center for the Performing Arts (Washington, DC). What makes this project unique when compared to the work of the MIT Media Lab, is that it is approached from the perspective of a music education specialist who desires to see technological innovation find a place among the current curricular offerings in music education. In some ways all of humanity can be viewed as possessing "special needs," and some of these new technologies make customizable music education possible when employed by thoughtful and entrepreneurial music teachers. Randles, C. (2011). What is a good musician?: An examination of student beliefs. Arts Education Policy Review, 112(1), 1-8. Primary Research Question: What impact will the use of a specifically programmed musical application that utilizes the iPad's motion sensitive capabilities have on the ability of students with special needs to creatively and meaningfully engage with music in musical performance?

KEYWORDS

special needs, technology, creativity

AIMS

Rationale: Music education has focused for centuries on performing masterworks, with special focus on the few talented musicians who can technically execute music in this tradition. The iPad is a medium by which students can connect to a musical world that was off limits just a short time ago. The results of this work have the potential to be helpful to (1) all who are interested in transforming the future of music teaching and learning through the use of new technologies (including, of course, the iPad), and (2) those specifically interested in giving individuals with special needs the ability to perform music. While there has been a wealth of published research on children's creative products and processes, the creative work of special needs students has not yet been examined thoroughly.

METHODS

This was a multiple case study. I collected survey responses, conducted phone and face-to-face interviews, collected personal journal entries, and transcribed video recordings of class sessions. Students made music using various applications for sound production, including GarageBand, Cosmovox, and ThumbJam. I would make use of all of the audio/video tools at my disposal to present the essential components of this project for conference attendees, fellow researchers, and fellow practitioners. Sample: The population for this study consisted of students and parents of a class that met weekly in the Psychiatry building on the USF Tampa campus over the course of one semester. Parents were asked to be a part of the study because many of them attended classes with their child, and many of them understood and were able to provide another lens into the home musical environment and weekly routines of their child. Many wanted to make music or assist their child in making music, and so it made good sense to ask them some of the same questions as were asked students, as a form of data triangulation.

Outcomes

The outcomes of this research are at heart practical. However, the results point to conceptual and philosophical work on the nature of "special needs." Could it be that all of humanity has "special needs" that might be remedied through the use of innovative personalized music education opportunities, developed by thoughtful and entrepreneurial music teachers?

References

Randles, C. (2011). What is a good musician?: An examination of student beliefs. *Arts Education Policy Review*, 112(1), 1-8.

Randles, C. (2013). *Being an iPadist*. General Music Today.

Randles, C. (2010). The relationship of compositional experiences of high school instrumentalists to music self-concept. *Bulletin of the Council for Research in Music Education*, 9-20.

Vocalmetrics: exploring multiple dimensions of singing in early popular music recordings

▍ Felix Schönfeld

    TU Dresden, Faculty of Computer Science, Germany

▍ Tilo Hähnel

    The Franz Liszt School of Music Weimar, Dep. of. musicology Weimar | Jena, Germany

Abstract

When exploring large sets of data and seeking for a comprehensive understanding, data visualization generally helps making things more obvious or even revealing new insights. Analysing voice and singing in popular music in the USA from 1900 to 1960 in a funded research project, we developed a web tool called *Vocalmetrics*, which allows manoeuvring through a corpus of short and exemplary audio files, which had been rated in nine dimensions of vocal expression, namely vibrato, glissando, roughness, breathiness, articulation, off-beat frequency, rubato, loudness, and register emphasis. The newly developed tool helps the user focusing on all these dimensions, which is important not only for musicological reasons but also for educational purposes. Working with *Vocalmetrics*, students can make themselves familiar with the singing voice, its means of expression and relations between vocal expression, genre, time and many further dimensions. The tool allows for searching the co-occurrences of vocal dimensions as well as to relate vocal styles and metadata, such as genre, year, record label, title, and singer. Therefore, the tool is an intuitive and playful way of exploring voice and singing in music.

Keywords

music education, data visualisation, singing

AIMS

We aim at classifying vocal characteristics of singers and genre-related singing styles. Therefore we created a data set composed of audio snippets, spectral views and ratings of different characteristics of vocal expression. With the help of a visualisation tool we expect to explore different characteristics of vocal expression more easily. Furthermore, the visualisation tool should help to analyse different characteristics of vocal expression in terms of their co-occurrences, genre-affiliation and development over time. When exploring a large database of exemplary audio-files, each of the file should be played back and visualised according to its vocal characteristics. Additionally, important metadata such as the singer's name, the title of the track, the year of recording, the record label and the genre must be included, too.

METHODS

The visualisation tool uses geometric visualization techniques to transform the data from vocal analyses into meaningful visual information. It satisfies both a specialist's and a learner's needs by using classical mathematical data representations as well as metaphor-based interaction concepts. Additionally, it supports the maintenance of individual data in the database by using direct manipulation techniques right within the visualization itself and even provides automatic mechanisms for helping the user when rating the vocal dimensions of new or existing music recordings.

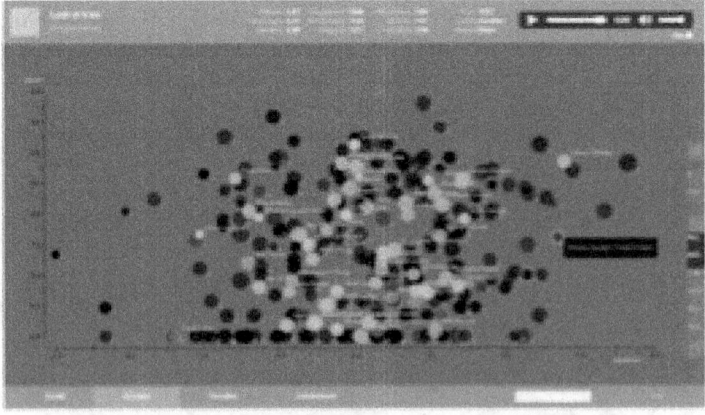

Outcomes

We released a web application based on up-to-date web technologies such as HTML5, CSS3 and SVG. It is executable in any modern browser and supports installation in both a local and a server environment. All that makes it is easy to get another new project started, either in private or in public field such as educational institutions.

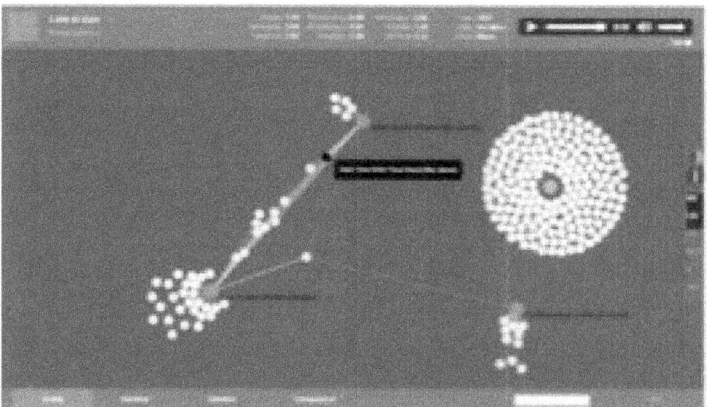

Acknowledgements

This research was funded by the German Research Foundation DFG.

Processes of Learning in the Project Studio

▍ Mark Slater
    University of Hull, UK

ABSTRACT

The emergence of the project studio is a story of increasing access to ever more powerful technologies that allow music to be produced in increasingly diverse circumstances. Proliferation of technologies capable of supporting musical creativity leads to a proliferation of creative practices across socio-demographic and geographic planes. Given this context, how do people learn what they need to know to produce their music? Music technologies and specialist programmes are now well established in the music education landscape, but for those making music in project studios set up in the spare bedroom, attic or garage, acquiring knowledge and developing skills often takes place outside formal institutions and curricula. Derived from a longitudinal research project tracing the life of a collaborative studio project that produced a form of popular music over an eight-year period, this paper will elucidate the mechanisms through which participants learn what they need to know, as they need to know it, in the project studio. In addition to analysing the qualitative data from this case study, existing education research clustering around informal and formal learning styles is interrogated to conclude, along with others, that such a binary view needs to be abandoned in favour of a more nuanced perspective. The collapse of any clear distinction between so-called formal and informal is propagated by the same technology that facilitates the kind of creative music practices I explore in its ability to provide access to tools, information, materials and communities. By re-categorising a selection of existing constructs that describe informal and formal learning styles, I propose five dimensions of learning (intentionality, agency, patterning, experience/concept and socio-architectural) and illustrate these using evidence from the studio project case study. These dimensions provide a descriptive framework. The case study evidence provides an insight into *what* is being learned (technological expertise, technical skills, socio-logistical skills and musical idiolect) along with *how* this learning takes place (encounter, exchange, enculturation and experimentalism). In summary, this paper will provide insight into an increasingly prevalent context of musical creativity (the domestic project studio) while proposing a refreshed framework for how we might describe styles and processes of learning.

Keywords

Project studio, Learning, Music production

Aims

To understand how people learn what they need to know, as they need to know it, in the project studio context; to formulate a framework for describing learning styles and processes; to give insight into a particular case study of collaborative musical creativity in the project studio.

Methods

Data were collected via participant diaries and semi-structured interviews throughout a period of the studio project's operation. These data were analysed according to principles of thematic identification derived from interpretative phenomenological analysis.

Outcomes

(Summary) Highlights the domestic project studio as a prevalent locus of music-making practices; identifies what skills and knowledge might be required by people making music with music technologies (in combination with or as opposed to musical instruments); proposes five dimensions of learning as derived from existing education literature to provide a refreshed perspective on the false dichotomy of informal-formal learning; offers four overall processes to explain how participants are acquiring necessary skills and knowledge.

Implications

(Summary) Invites further consideration of studio-based creative practices; challenges notions of situated learning styles; suggests processes derived from a particular form of music-making practice that might flow into pedagogical praxis.

REFERENCES

Cain, T. (2013). "Passing It On": Beyond Formal or Informal Pedagogies. *Music Education Research*, 15, 74–91.

Jenkins, P. (2011). Formal and Informal Music Educational Practices. *Philosophy of Music Education Review*, 19, 179–97.

Théberge, P. (2004). The Network Studio: Historical and Technological Paths to a New Ideal in Music Making. *Social Studies of Science*, 34, 759–81.

Picalab Musi-Matemáticas Sonoras Interactivas. Design, implementation and evaluation of a software package and didactic guides for mathematical education based on musical metaphors for primary education in Chile

▌ Jesús Tejada

    Universidad de Valencia, Spain

▌ Tomás Thayer

    Universidad Metropolitana de Ciencias de la Educación, Chile

▌ Alicia Venegas

    Universidad Metropolitana de Ciencias de la Educación, Chile

▌ Randall Ledermann

    Universidad Metropolitana de Ciencias de la Educación, Chile

▌ Alberto Lecaros

    Universidad Metropolitana de Ciencias de la Educación, Chile

▌ Mirko Petrovich

    Universidad Metropolitana de Ciencias de la Educación, Chile

Abstract

The Picalab Project proposes the design, development, and study of an integrated mathematics-music software solution to leverage learning of mathematics in a classroom context, by use of music as metaphors for mathematical curricular contents. Software modules were developed, based on Brousseau's Theory of Didactical Situations framework, and aimed at the 3rd, 4th and 5th grades of Chilean primary education level.

The modules can be used by students all by themselves, but the teacher is considered a primary and key player in the implementation of this solution. Primary proof of concept and usability tests seem to point to music, as representation of curricular mathematical contents acts as scaffolding of learning, anchors new information in the socio-cultural context of learning, can be part of situated knowledge, and offers a new perspective for learning mathematics at schools, giving pupils opportunities to develop their own mental representations

Keywords

mathematical learning, didactic software, music

Aims

The objective of the Picalab project is to design MMSI (Musical Mathematical Sound Interactive) modules, consisting of a software application paired with a didactic guide, which would allow a school teacher to present mathematical concepts or concepts, leveraged on a musical or sound based experience. Great consideration was given to the fact that Math teachers do not necessarily have sufficient training in music, and could therefore be averted by the apprehension of having to address musical concepts they do not master during their lessons with the MMSI. To this end, a didactic guide was specifically written to show the teacher how to best take advantage of the interest that students naturally have in music and sound, to create a significant contextualization for otherwise abstract or difficult mathematical concepts

Methods

The production of MMSI consists of a three stage, iterative process: 1) Proposals for a non-functional prototype; 2) Selection and prototype implementation; and 3) Class evaluation and feedback.

Outcomes

Preliminary results show that students become highly motivated with this approach. Students show a very good attitude towards the modules, and remain in activities for the whole extent of the class. Most remarkable, is the fact that they can engage in active discussions about topics that, in a typical lecture format, they do not. They engage in formulating hypothesis regarding the "behavior" of different multiples, and then proceed to validate or reject them by means of the module itself. They consistently arrive at conclusions such as "a common multiple of two numbers is necessarily the product of these numbers", and shortly discover that this is not necessarily the least common multiple. The fact that these abstract or non-contextualized math topics are now presented in a musical context is apparently a key factor. This is currently being tested for later publication

CONCLUSIONS

revealed a very important motivation and positive attitude towards the use of each music-mathematic module presented, particularly in those with a more game-like form. The music component, most evident in the exploratory (no guided) first phase of use of each module, is attractive to practically all students, even those that do not consider themselves "music experts". Equally important, this interest and motivation is also present towards the mathematical concepts involved. The fact that these are presented in a musical context seems to enhance interest and scaffold comprehension in them.These preliminary results seem to indicate that this interdisciplinary approach is worthy of further research, which we expect to broaden as we gather more and definitive data in the quantitative and qualitative final assessment

ACKNOWLEDGEMENTS

This study has been granted by Fondo de Fomento al Desarrollo Científico y Tecnológico (FONDEF, code TE10I010), Chilean national agency dependent of CONICYT (National Council for Science and Technology)"

REFERENCES

Puckette, M. (1996). Pure Data. *Proceedings of the International Computer Music Conference*. San Francisco: International Computer Music Association.

Brousseau G. (1998). *Théorie des Situations Didactiques*. Grenoble: La Pensée Sauvage.

Wollenberg, Susan (2003). Music and mathematics: an overview. In John Fauvel, Raymond Flood and Robin Wilson (eds.) *Music and Mathematics. From Pythagoras to Fractals*. Oxford: Oxford University Press.

Connecting learners, employers and practitioners through emergent digital technology

Mark Thorley

Coventry University, UK

Abstract

The major impact of technology upon music composition, production and consumption has shifted from production tools (the project studio, DAWs etc.), to the digital technologies which facilitate the digital distribution and streaming of music. This has altered the commercial landscape (and therefore, the skills needed) for music practitioners, recording studios and record companies amongst many others. The traditional barrier between music composer or producer and the audience has been bridged by emergent digital technologies, and there are now many ways in which music can be showcased, demonstrated, shared or collaborated upon. These same facilitating technologies offer a significant opportunity for learners (and therefore, educators) particularly where the aim is to develop capability in composing or producing music in the expectation of working in the 'real world'. Despite this, (and possibly for cultural and structural reasons), the potential associated with adopting such technology is largely unrealised in educational contexts. This is particularly surprising given the push towards Employer/Higher Education Partnership by the Higher Education Funding Council for England, a general increased emphasis upon the skills required for employment (Dawes and Jewell, 2005), and the documented difficulty which students have in articulating their skills to the outside world (Brown, 2007). This paper describes the realisation and outcomes of a project funded by the UK's Higher Education Academy (HEA) designed to embed employer and practitioner involvement in the development and assessment of final year Music Technology portfolios. The rationale and methodology (project realisation and research examination) are described before turning to an examination of the key outcomes which have found application nationally and internationally in a variety of disciplinary contexts.

KEYWORDS

Music Composition and Creation, Music Production, Assessment

AIMS

The project (funded by the HEA) aimed to establish the feasibility and impact of embedding employer/practitioner involvement in the development and assessment of Music Technology final year portfolios. This took place using emergent digital tools which facilitate the showcasing, demonstration of, and collaboration around music as well as video and e-portfolio technology. Inevitably, it also included the full gamut of technological tools commonly used in composition, recording and production. This paper aims to show the rationale, the potential and realisation of such an approach. It also aims to outline the key outcomes which have found cross-discipline application nationally and internationally, and the risk factors associated with this approach.

METHODS

The project realisation took place in a Personal Development Planning (PDP) module within the Music and Creative Technologies Programme at Coventry University. The input of employers/practitioners took place at two key stages – before development of the portfolio, and afterwards. The concept was therefore that of the employers/practitioners 'informing' portfolio development and assessing the work from a 'real world' perspective. The interactions were enabled using digital tools typified by e-portfolios, audio sharing and showcasing technologies, video sharing sites and social media. Content was also produced using the typical tools of music composition and production (analogue and digital). Dissemination of the project was a requirement of the funding, so an appropriate research methodology was agreed by the HEA. This took a participant observation approach outlined by Manis and Meltzer (1967). Additionally, such an approach was appropriate as the researcher needed to act as a 'research instrument', interpreting the very different worlds of undergraduate students and the high profile industry professionals. The impact upon the student work was examined together with the impact upon the student experience before investigating the impact upon the employers/practitioners involved.

Outcomes

Several changes were observed and measured from the academic's point of view. Firstly, participation and engagement in the module improved compared with the same module in previous years and other concurrent modules. Secondly, level of understanding of the professional environment was improved as seen in the quality of the submitted work. A deeper appreciation of the breadth of skills and knowledge was observed ranging from a better coverage of job functions through to improved quality of targeted evidence of capability (sound files, compositions, assignments etc.). Impact upon the student experience was also significant. Students commented positively before the experience via social media and afterwards through module evaluation and focus groups. Specifically, they gained perspectives which would not be learnt by any other method as it was done in partnership with the employers/practitioners. Additionally, their aspiration was raised by the work being assessed by outside parties. Lastly, there were significant effects on the employers/practitioners involved. Through the experience, they became better able to understand how new entrants into the music industry develop technical and creative skills, interface with technology and face the challenge of transition into professional life. This placed them in a better position to recruit (or contract) new entrants to the industry. They did, however, have significant initial difficulty getting to grips with the assessment of student work.

Implications

The innovative approach taken to embed employers/practitioners in the development and assessment of final year Music Technology portfolios resulted in better engagement and a level of appreciation of skills and knowledge which was deeper and more significantly applied. The involvement of the employers/practitioners facilitated a 'partnership' learning approach with the learners. These concepts have seen the model being adopted internationally in US institutions, other Music Technology (and related discipline) courses in the UK, and in other disciplines in the host institution. As a model then, it can be applied in Music Technology Education (and other disciplines) where developing (and articulating) creative, technical and transferable skills to employers is crucial but challenging. The most significant challenge is in finding appropriate employers/practitioners who ideally, as well as being leaders in their field are able and willing to take the time to articulate their roles, to understand and undertake assessment and be appreciative of the needs of learners. There is, however, risk in allowing employers/practitioners to form judgements on an institution from student work. Utilising new technology in assessment also involves some risk.

ACKNOWLEDGEMENTS

This project was funded by the Higher Education Academy and Coventry University.

REFERENCES

Brown, R (2007). Enhancing Student Employability?: Current practice and student experiences in HE Performing Arts. *Arts and Humanities in Higher Education*, 6(1); 28-49.

Dawes, F and Jewell, M (2005). Creating Enterprise: Developing partnerships between Universities and Creative Industries. Paper presented to the *Creative Enterprise in Higher Education Conference*, PALENTINE, Lancaster University.

Manis, J G and Meltzer B N (1967). *Symbolic Interactionism: A Reader in Social Psychology*. Boston: Allyn and Bacon.

How could musicology help me become a better record producer?: tensions between the vocational and the theoretical in music pedagogy

Simon Zagorski-Thomas

London College of Music, University of West London, UK

Abstract

There is a fundamental schism in higher education between the vocational and the theoretical that is characterised as much by ideology and convention as by content and structure. Music is no exception and, in the field of record production where creative practice intersects with the social construction and employment of technology, it is common to hear educators with a practitioner background dismissing aspects of the musicology of record production as being purely descriptive and of no practical value. Whilst there is obvious value in documenting the social history and technical practices of music making as an archival process, the question arises as to how vocational education can use theory to do more than simply pass on the existing conventions of good practice. This paper provides two practical case studies that explore issues raised in a chapter for the forthcoming Music, Technology & Education: Critical Perspectives (King & Himonides, 2014). The first relates to an example of Practice As Research whereby a PhD student is developing a broader understanding of the nature of tacit knowledge through an exploration of practice using late 1960s recording hardware. The second case study looks at the practical application and pedagogical implications of a research project that is starting to look at how conceptual terms such as 'heavy', 'big', 'light' or 'spacious' might be explored through particular schematic features and their relationship to audio processing techniques. Both of these case studies relate to the challenges within vocational pedagogy in higher education that go beyond high level technical training and seek to enable students to think about the process of record production and the interpretation of recorded music in abstract and theoretical terms and to develop their own creative strategies and techniques.

Keywords

Record Production, Vocational Pedagogy,

Aims

This paper aims to use two case studies of current research activity in the field of record production to explore new directions in vocational pedagogy. They will specifically address the question of how students can be given conceptual tools that allow them to find solutions to creative problems that go beyond the existing conventions of good practice but don't go so far beyond the realities of the creative process that they can't envisage the practical applications.

Methods

These case studies will be analysed in terms of a theoretical framework that draws on ecological perception (Clarke 2005), embodied cognition (Lakoff & Johnson 2003) and the social construction of technology (Pinch et al. 2012). Indeed the theoretical framework provides a model that encompasses both the ways in which practitioners and participants produce and interpret recorded music and also the ways in which students acquire knowledge through the education system and synthesise new knowledge.

Outcomes

In many ways, this project's title reflects the ongoing ambitions of the Association for the Study of the Art of Record Production: to resolve the tensions between vocational and theoretical approaches to the study of record production and to build bridges between them. As such, these outcomes are merely staging posts on that bigger journey. Nonetheless, these case studies provide concrete examples of the ideas floated in a more theoretical chapter to be published shortly (Himonides & King 2014).

Discussion

The presentation will conclude with a discussion of the problems of maintaining the balance between the requirements of vocational pedagogy and the demands for critical thinking in the higher education system.

BIBLIOGRAPHY

Clarke, E.F. (2005). *Ways of Listening: An Ecological Approach to the Perception of Musical Meaning*, Oxford University Press, USA.

King, A. & Himonides, E. eds. (2014). *Music, Technology & Education: Critical Perspectives*, Farnham: Ashgate Publishing Limited.

Lakoff, G. & Johnson, M. (2003). *Metaphors We Live By 2nd ed.*, University Of Chicago Press.

Pinch, T., Bijker, W.E. & Hughes, T.P. eds. (2012). *The Social Contruction of Technological Systems: New Directions in the sociology and History of Technology Anniversary.* Cambridge, MA: MIT Press.

REFERENCES

Clarke, E.F. (2005) Ways of Listening: An Ecological Approach to the Perception of Musical Meaning, Oxford: Oxford University Press

Lakoff, G. & Johnson, M. (2003) Metaphors We Live By Chicago: University Of Chicago Press

Pinch, T., Bijker, W.E. & Hughes, T.P. eds. (2012) The Social Contruction of Technological Systems: New Directions in the sociology and History of Technology Cambridge, MA: MIT Press

Critical Insights

www.ingramcontent.com/pod-product-compliance
Lightning Source LLC
Chambersburg PA
CBHW061449300426
44114CB00014B/1899